BFI TELEVISION MONOGRAPH

10

Everyday Television: *Nationwide*

Charlotte Brunsdon
David Morley

produced by
The British Film Institute
Educational Advisory Service

British Film Institute
127 Charing Cross Road, London WC2H 0EA
1978

This study of the BBC's *Nationwide* attempts to produce a 'reading' of the programme which reveals the ways in which it constructs an image of its audience. Specifically, the study details the methods through which the programme addresses itself both to a national audience, united in the diversity of its regions, and an audience of ordinary individuals, grouped in families: everyday television for everyday people.

The authors

Charlotte Brunsdon is a research student and David Morley a research associate at the Centre for Contemporary Cultural Studies, University of Birmingham.

Printed in England by Brown Knight & Truscott Ltd, London and Tonbridge

Contents

Acknowledgements

We should like to thank Nadine Cartner for taking the photographs and the BBC for permission to use them. We are also grateful to the BBC and Michael Barratt for permission to publish the transcript in Chapter 3.

Preface

The work on which this monograph is based was originally carried out collectively by the Media Group at the Centre for Contemporary Cultural Studies, University of Birmingham, in the period 1975–6. Its members were: Roz Brody, Charlotte Brunsdon, Ian Connell, Stuart Hall, Bob Lumley, Richard Nice, Roy Peters. This work was discussed by the group and individuals wrote up contributions on different aspects of the programme. Since then, we have worked from this material to produce the present monograph, incorporating some of the writing produced at the first stage, although sometimes in relation to different problems from those originally addressed. The Media Group have all read and commented on this work at different stages, and in this context we are particularly grateful to Stuart Hall. We would also like to thank Ed Buscombe for his help.

Our analysis focuses on the ideological themes articulated in the programme, only partially relating these to their material bases in the formal properties of the discourse, and we have not integrated the visual level of the analysis into the central argument – this is one of the most obvious limitations of the work. We have also found ourselves, at times, wanting to make arguments for which we do not have sufficient data because of the different ways in which problems were originally posed. This has happened, for example, in relation to questions concerning women and the family, which were not focused originally as major concerns, but which have come to occupy a more explicit space in the analysis. It has frequently been a case of recognising only at a later stage what questions should have been asked of the material in order to produce satisfactory data.

The *Nationwide* programme examined in some detail in chapter 3 of this monograph has subsequently been used within a research project, funded by the British Film Institute, on 'the encoding and decoding moments in television discourse and programming'; this has been under way at the Centre for Contemporary Cultural Studies since September 1976. This work constitutes an attempt to explore the range of differential decodings of the programme arrived at by individuals and groups in different socio-cultural locations. Within the context of the larger study, then, the programme analysis presented here constitutes the base line against which differential readings may be posed, and our reading of the programme will be open to modification in the light of the audience work.

C.B.
D.M.

1 Going *Nationwide*

(i)   Nation and Regions: the historical development of the programme

(ii) The world of *Nationwide*: the *Mandala*

(iii) Programme format and slot

(iv) The *Nationwide* style of presentation

(v)   The material of *Nationwide*: specificity of news values

(i) Nation and Regions: the historical development of the programme

Nationwide was started in 1966 as part of a strategy adopted by the BBC to meet three different needs. First, there was the necessity to build on the 'spot' established by *Tonight*, and to produce a programme which would carry through the solid audiences for the early regional news into BBC1's major evening output beginning at 7 p.m. On the other hand, there was the need to meet the criticism that the BBC output was too much dominated by the metropolis and thus failed to express/deal adequately with the needs of 'the regions'. The 'regionalism' of *Nationwide* was seen as a necessary basis for any sense of national unity in the conditions of the late 60s and 70s – or, as the BBC evidence to Annan put it:

> local and regional services are an essential part of a truly national broadcasting system. (BBC *Handbook* 1978.)

Finally, there were the recommendations made by the McKinsey Report and developed in the BBC policy document, *Broadcasting in the 70s*, that fuller use should be made of the company's regional studios, allowing for regional specialisation and a 'rationalisation' of resources (and cost-effectiveness).

The regional element has always been crucial to *Nationwide* – the idea:

> is to impress on the viewer that this is a programme which is not dominated by London and which embraces every main centre in the UK. (William Hardcastle reviewing current affairs schedules; quoted in Connell 1975.)

So much so that when *Nationwide* 'looked at London' in the film 'Our Secret Capital' (*Nationwide* 16/8/76) Julian Pettifer, the presenter, consciously acknowledged the programme's brief by saying:

> On *Nationwide* we try desperately not to be a metropolitan programme. Tonight is an exception. For the next 25 minutes we're looking at life in London: but we offer no excuse, because after all, wherever you live in the UK, London is your capital ...

Similarly Stuart Wilkinson (deputy editor of *Nationwide*) claimed that:

> *Nationwide* would not be a nationwide programme without this facility to involve our colleagues in the regions. The crosstalk between the regions is the very essence of the programme. (Quoted in Brody 1976, p. 20.)

The programme attempts to construct a close and 'homely' relationship with its regionally differentiated audiences: this can be seen clearly in the programme's self-presentation, or billing, in the *Radio Times*:

Reporting England: Look North, South Today, Look East, Midlands Today, Points West, Spotlight South West. (*Radio Times* 29/3/77.)

Today's news and views in your corner of England presented by the BBC's regional newsrooms. Then . . . take a look at the scene *Nationwide*. (*Radio Times* 13/1/76.)

. . . present news and views in your region tonight. Then at 6.22 . . . present some of the more interesting stories of life in today's Britain . . . (*Radio Times* 14/1/76.)

News and views in your region tonight. Then the national scene, presented by . . . (*Radio Times* 15/1/76.)

. . . present the British scene to the people of Britain . . . (*Radio Times* 16/1/76.)

Nationwide is positively involved in the search for regional variety: of customs and ways of life. Indeed 'Let's go *Nationwide* . . . and see what the regions think . . .' becomes the characteristic *Nationwide* form of presentation. Thus the programme is able to stress regional differences (different dishes, superstitions, competitions), to present a Nation composed of variety and diversity, but also to unify the regions in the face of National Crises: 'How is Leeds coping with the drought? What about the South-West?' (17/8/76.)

We see variations in regional responses to issues given by the centre: classically, regional variations in the celebration of the Jubilee. But the regional is still contained within the national: regionalism is the life-blood of *Nationwide*, but full-blooded separatist or nationalist movements – such as the Irish Republican Movement – transgress the limits of the *Nationwide* discourse, breaking as they do the assumed frame of the 'United Kingdom'.

Similarly, within the programme, the links over to regions are usually from London, and are used to 'fill out' regional aspects of something of national import; the regions do not usually initiate stories. The regions follow, and are linked to the national news – they pick up stories signalled in the national news and flesh out their significance for the region. The input of 'regional stories' – material drawn from the 'life of the region' – is subordinate to this 'national with regional effects' input; the regional variations are orchestrated from the central London studio base. London is the 'absent' region, the invisible bearer of national unity. It is both technologically and ideologically the heart of the programme.

(ii) **The world of** *Nationwide***: the** *Mandala*

During the period in which we viewed the programme, *Nationwide* regularly opened with the use of a specially designed graphic device – a lengthy sequence in which the basic concentric patterns altered through the superimposition of different images, ending in an abstract which culminated in the programme title. This device was based on the *Mandala*, an oriental mystical symbol of the universe. In its original form, various aspects of the life of *samsara* (the cycle of birth and death) or religious representations of the deity were depicted. *Mandala* is a Sanskrit word meaning 'magic circle' and its basic pattern is a set of concentrically arranged figures with radial or spherical emblems arranged around a central point. It was the term which Frank Bough used to describe the opening sequence of the programme. (See figs. 1–3.)

Deprived of its celestial resonance, the *Mandala* which heads *Nationwide* does seem to have a similar function to the Buddhist version. It suggests that 'all human life is there' – tied together at the central point ('the still point of the turning world') which is, of course, *Nationwide* itself. The device does symbolise something which is essential to the programme – unity in diversity. The form of the device – both the way the images work and the accompanying music – represent something of how the programme sees itself: the whole introduction can be read as a meta-discourse about the programme itself. The wheel suggests constant movement around the country – surveying everything of interest. The points of the compass index its outward, regional viewpoint – each wheel being representative of the various *Nationwide* regions. But the device – like the programme itself – is centered – everything flowing out of and returning to a single source.

The basic pattern of the *Nationwide Mandala*, then, consists of a set of turning wheels whose movement emanates from a central source. The abstract pattern is then followed by a set of tone images, in which are depicted something of the range and variety of topics to be dealt with by the programme. The fact that the screen is occupied at any one time by more than one image produces a split-screen effect – connoting both the simultaneity of 'things going on' at any one time, but also, as the images play off against and between one another, setting up a play of inter-textuality between the various signs. After the initial sequence, at least one spot is occupied at any one time by a *Nationwide* reporter or presenter, suggesting that these multifarious aspects of our national life are brought to you, the viewers, by 'our' men and women in the field. These reporters are given by *Nationwide*, and signified in the *Mandala* as occupying, a privileged 'overseeing' role in relation to the actuality events depicted in the other wheels. Hence, the attention is also drawn towards the programme's mediating role – we see, know about and participate in events through the crucial intervention in the field of the presenters who act as go-betweens, like 'fences' between us and the world. It is the presence of the reporters, plus the pattern of the device itself, which holds everything together in this opening sequence. The reporters constitute *Nationwide's* effective repertorial unity. The long arm of the *Nationwide* team is seen to stretch into every corner of our lives to gather material for us and bring it back to the 'home' base.

(iii) Programme format and slot

The magazine format of *Nationwide* – short items (rarely longer than 10 minutes), light relief mixed in with 'heavy fare' to hold the viewers' attention – 'the Postmaster General mixed with a tattooed cat' (quoted in Gillman 1975) – is to some extent determined by the slot that the programme occupies: the break between children's TV and the BBC's major evening output. The programme is usually followed by light entertainment, family shows, quizzes or the like – it is a time of evening when, as Michael Bunce (one-time editor of *Nationwide*) put it:

> people have had a hard day's work and when they sit down they don't want a remorseless, demanding, hard tack diet every night. (Gillman 1975.)

There is, therefore, a deliberate policy in *Nationwide* to include light items, especially when the programme contains some 'heavy fare'. Barratt argues:

> We need some light relief if we are to hold the viewer's interest: there's a limit to the serious fare they can absorb or want to at this time of evening. (Quoted in Brody 1976.)

These 'common sense' definitions of the nature of the 'slot' – when people are coming in from work, when the whole family including children will be present, when no sustained attention is possible, etc., allow us to construct *Nationwide's* own sense of its responsibilities and its constituency.

The space from 6 to 7 p.m. does tend also to be populated by domestic serials, comedies, panel games, and *Nationwide* is 'contaminated' by, or actively parasitic upon, these alternative genres, as well as aspects of the time zone preceding the early evening news, that reserved for children's programes. Thus the history of the time slot makes available a certain range of genres which all have a common sense appropriateness to that hour of the day. This is the basis for some of *Nationwide's* quality of heterogeneity and also for the oscillations of tone within some of the items.

(iv) The *Nationwide* style of presentation

In his autobiography, Barratt spells out a key element in the '*Nationwide* Style':

> The art of communication on any topic – whether it be life itself, or the price of porridge – demands the use of easily understood words, and is greatly heightened by skilful illustration. (Quoted in Brody 1976, p. 24.)

The stress is on direct and effective communication – 'simple language, common language if you like' (Michael Barratt) – getting it across to the people. Thus, when 'heavy' items are dealt with, *Nationwide* is primarily concerned to 'establish the point at the heart of the matter' and concentrate on getting that over, unlike, for instance, *Panorama*, which, after 'establishing the topic', will explore the different perspectives and dimensions of it, offering a range of views and definitions for the audience's 'education'. (Cf., Connell et al. 1976.)

The discourse of *Nationwide* then is relatively closed; the stress on 'making the issues comprehensible', translating them into 'real terms', leaves little space for interpretation. The endeavour for *Nationwide* is to establish the time/place/status/immediacy of events and people involved in them – making these, where possible, concrete and personalised – and to get the 'main point' of an item across to the audience.

In *Nationwide* there is a thread almost of anti-intellectualism; 'experts' are held in some value for what they may have to contribute, but it all has to be translatable into the language of immediate issues and everyday concerns.

Thus, while experts expound on 'the causes of inflation', the *Nationwide* team do their best to find out what inflation really means, how it will affect 'our' day-to-day living, whether anything can be done about it ('Yes, minister, but how will that improve the situation here tomorrow . . .'). The team often expresses 'our' exasperation with politicians by asking them 'down to earth' questions. This can be seen in the different interviewing styles of *Nationwide* and *Panorama*; a *Panorama* interview with the Chancellor will tend to probe and challenge his position with reference to the positions of opposing political parties and economic experts. The challenge put by *Nationwide* interviewers will tend much more to be at the level of practical policy making: 'will it help/work?' and will often take the form of a 'common sensical' perspective in terms of which politicians of all parties are likely to be seen as culpable. This style of interviewing is directly in the tradition of *Tonight* and its style of popular journalism – once described as the 'discipline of entertainment':

> We are flippant, irreverent, disbelieving when we feel we should be; we refuse to be taken in by pompous spokesmen . . . (Cliff Michelmore, introducing the programme after summer break, 1961.)

Implicit in this perspective is a populist ideology which takes for granted the irrelevance of 'politics' to the real business of everyday life ('Whichever party is in power I'll still not have a job. Prices will still rise . . .') and also takes for granted the disillusionment of the electorate with 'politicians' and their promises.

The 'serious issues' – unemployment, inflation, etc. – which are the basis of most current affairs programming, can therefore only enforce attention within the *Nationwide* discourse where they can be shown to have immediate effects on everyday life; when this happens *Nationwide* can wheel in Robert McKenzie and his clipboard and graphics to tell us what this 'IMF loan business' is all about. But, even on such occasions, everyday life and its continuities (nature, sport, entertainment, quirky events) are, within the

Nationwide world, what 'frame' these issues, and are called upon (reassuringly) to put them into perspective. ('And on this gloomy day, a look on the brighter side' ... 'With all this crisis going on one could almost have forgotten that today was Shrove Tuesday'...)

Barratt, the principal anchorman during the period of viewing, presents himself as the embodiment of this 'populist' perspective: a no-nonsense man of the people, stressing down-to-earth common sense, not only by asking questions he thinks the public would want to ask but also, unlike many other current affairs presenters, by adding comments ('Well, they do seem rather daft reasons for going on strike ...' *Nationwide* 14/3/73) he assumes the public might make, or at least agree with.

Interestingly, these comments are not seen to transgress the requirements of balance and impartiality. They rest on an image of 'the people' *outside* the structures of politics and government. Precisely because they are made from a perspective at odds with that of parliamentary politics – 'the politicians' as such are suspect from this perspective – these comments do not favour the position of one party against another within that framework. This 'common-sense' critique of 'politics' presents itself as a-political, despite the obviously political content of common-sense wisdom about what 'we all know ...' The discourse of *Nationwide*, rooted as it is in this populist 'everyday' perspective on events, undercuts the traditional discourse of parliamentary politics by basing its criticisms on a set of assumptions about 'what everybody thinks'. It is a discourse which poses 'ordinary people' as its source, and thus re-presents historically-determined and necessarily political positions simply as a set of natural, taken-for-granted 'home truths'.

Moreover, the *Nationwide* perspective is legitimated not only through its identification with the content of common-sense wisdom, but also through the forms of discourse in which that perspective is constructed. *Nationwide* employs a kind of populist 'ventriloquism' (Smith 1975, p. 67) which enables the programme to speak with the voice of the people; *i.e.,* to mirror and reproduce the voice of its own audience. *Nationwide* adopts the language of popular speech – the language is always concrete, direct and punchy, with an assumption of and a reference to always pre-existing 'knowledge'. This populist vocabulary is the language of 'common sense' which the programme adopts and transforms, picking up popular terms of speech (much in the style of the *Daily Mirror*'s 'Come off it Harold ...'), mimicking phrases and clichés, and putting them to new uses, making them carry the weight of a political message. *Nationwide* often uses, and sometimes inverts, proverbs and clichés, quite self-consciously (the 'postcard shot' of Blackpool; 'when in Rome let the Romans do as you do', 19/5/76; etc.) – grounding its vocabulary in familiar tags and sentence constructions. ('This may look like a load of old rubbish to you ...', 19/4/76.) The 'persona' of the programme, then, is a professionally formulated reconstruction based in and on 'popular speech' and its sedimented wisdoms. The use of this linguistic register is one of the ways in which *Nationwide* constructs 'ordinary people' as the subject of its particular kind of speech.

This 'populist ventriloquism' is a crucial strand in the way the programme attempts to forge an 'identification' with its audience; its project is to be accepted by the audience as their representative, speaking for them, and speaking to them from a perspective, and in a language, which they share. At the same time, this work of constructing identifications is actively denied in the programme: the presenters appear as 'just like us', just ordinary people – who happen to be 'on telly', doing the talking, while we listen.

The tendency of *Nationwide* to repress the work of producing its own discourse is nowhere so clearly evident as in the way the programme presents itself in the *Radio Times*:

Britain's nightly mirror to the face of Britain. (29/3/77.)

presenting a mirror to the face of Britain. (1/4/77.)

Richard Stilgoe reflecting ideas and opinions from the postbag. (1/11/76.)

Nationwide, in short, offers us a 'nightly mirror [rather than a window] on the world'. It presents itself as catching in its varied and comprehensive gaze 'everything' which could possibly be of interest to us, and simply 'mirrors' or reflects it back to us. What is more, it 'sees' these events in exactly the same perspective, and speaks of them in exactly the same 'voice', as that of its audience. Everything in *Nationwide* works so as to support this mirror-structure of reflections and recognitions. The ideology of television as a transparent medium – simply showing us 'what is happening' – is raised here to a high pitch of self-reflexivity. The whole of the complex work of the production of *Nationwide*'s version of 'reality', sustained by the practices of recording, selecting, editing, framing and linking, and the identificatory strategies of producing 'the scene, *Nationwide*', is repressed in the programme's presentation of itself as an unproblematic reflection of 'us' and 'our world' in 'our' programme. *Nationwide* thus naturalises its own practice, while at the same time it is constantly engaged in constituting the audience in its own image. It makes the object of its discourse and practice – the audience – the subject of its speech. The discourse of *Nationwide* thus depends on its ability constantly to reconstruct this imaginary equivalence, this perfect transparency, between the 'us' who are seen and the 'we' who see. What we 'see' and recognise is a reflection of ourselves and our world, caught in the mirror-structure of the screen.

(v) The material of *Nationwide*: specificity of news values

Nationwide is a 'mosaic made up of a variety of interests' where the viewer does not know if s/he will see 'a film of Ulster or a beer-drinking snail' because *Nationwide* has 'no brief other than to be unpredictable, informative and entertaining'. (Quoted in Gillman 1975.) This is the territory originally 'mapped out' for current affairs TV by *Tonight*:

> *Tonight*'s back ... the familiar bouncy tune will invite you to look around (with Cliff Michelmore and his team) at the topical, the insignificant, the provocative, and even the sentimental issues of the day. Such is the range of the programme that no string of adjectives will suffice to make a boundary of its activities. (*Radio Rimes* 26/8/60.)

Nationwide must be topical, but its material is not the same as the material of the national news. While news programming usually acts as a baseline for current affairs TV there is always a selective translation from the domain of news into that of current affairs; current affairs programmes differing according to whether they have a closer or more distant relation to news output. Items usually have to 'pass through' the news before becoming suitable topics for current affairs TV, but not all news items will survive the transition. For instance 'crime', which is routinely 'news', will only become current affairs material if it involves some special feature, or if the crimes are seen to form some significant and problematic social pattern (such as 'mugging').

The differential relations of current affairs TV to news can be seen, for example, by comparing *Tonight* Mark II – which has a close relationship to news, routinely taking up and developing the immediate background to news items – with *Panorama*, which selects only the 'heavy items' (foreign policy, the budget, incomes policy, etc.) from the news.

Nationwide characteristically has a 'distanced' relation to the 'National News', although all the regional programmes carry local news in the traditional format. The 'newsworthy' items that *Nationwide* sets off against an always taken-for-granted reference point of normality are not those like the unexpected 'big bang' (News) or the world-shattering political development (*Panorama*) nor even the worrying deviant (social problem TV) but the extraordinary, perplexing various, eccentric quirks of otherwise ordinary people and their lives. *Nationwide* deals in 'human interest' stories. 'Heavy' items like Britain's involvement with the IMF, which are the staple diet of serious current affairs programmes (like *Panorama*), are explicitly featured only sporadically. These problems are, however, routinely recognised, even taken-for-granted, as the familiar background against which more typical *Nationwide* items are foregrounded. *Nationwide* items are often introduced with openers like 'In these days of economic crisis . . .'. When such items are handled, the 'angle' on them will be the search for 'the brighter side', 'what can be done', the 'good news among the bad'.

Nationwide policy in these issues, on the selection and handling of their material, is, at least in part, designed to respond to the fact that, as the BBC Audience Research Dept. Survey put it:

Four times as many people mentioned politics as mentioned any other subject as the 'most boring'.

What people wanted of a current affairs programme, according to the Survey, was:

> on the spot film, where the action is, to see for themselves ... to hear the people who are the subjects of the report telling their own story – not debates and discussions between experts in a TV studio.

Nationwide responds to these demands by placing first and foremost the 'discipline of entertainment' – the focus on the quirky, the fascinating, the sensational as a strategy for holding the attention of the audience, in order to lead them to the 'preferred reading' of a given event: the programme aims to produce 'interesting stories' which will 'grab the audience'. (*Nationwide* producer, quoted in Gillman 1975.) *Nationwide* doesn't cover areas remote from everyday life (like a *Panorama* special on Vietnam) but visits the places many of us have visited, takes us into the living rooms of ordinary families, shows us people enjoying their leisure time, couples coping with inflation and their new baby. The aim is to be 'a reflection of what you and your family talk about at the end of the day'. *Nationwide* thus occupies a peculiar space in the spectrum of current affairs TV; uniquely, on *Nationwide*, the majority of items are about ordinary people in their everyday lives. These items are always presented with a 'newsy' inflexion, but none the less they overwhelmingly draw their material from the 'normal/everyday' category which usually constitutes the absent baseline against which the 'newsworthiness' of other items is constituted.

It is from this area of 'everyday life' that *Nationwide* routinely produces the bulk of its magazine items: such as the story of the 'man who wrote out the Bible by hand'. (*Nationwide* 2/1/76.) Such stories could not in any sense become 'news' within the dominant current affairs framework of news values. However, these items are the specific constituency of *Nationwide*: the dominant perspective is reversed here. The items generated are from a 'grassroots' level: ordinary people's extraordinary habits/hobbies; or the effects of the state/bureaucracy as felt in the lives of 'ordinary folk' as it impinges on the sphere of private life.

Nationwide roots itself in the 'normal' and the everyday, in a 'consensus' based on what it represents as the 'natural' expectations of its audience. A vast proportion of *Nationwide* stories are simply about individuals 'like you or I', with their special skills and interests. Of course, a story about people doing absolutely ordinary things can't trigger an item on its own – even a magazine item – since it would contain no news potential whatsoever. The absolute norm is invisible in the perspective of news: it is what provides the taken for-granted background to everything else.

Nationwide, then, is grounded in the obvious, the familiar – but in celebrating this area of everyday life, the programme works on and against this 'norm'. *Nationwide* is constantly discovering that appearances are deceptive: the items often spotlight the special things that otherwise 'ordinary people' are doing. Here, *Nationwide* plays off a range of oppositions around the normal/abnormal, ordinary/eccentric polarities, discovering that the 'ordinary' is never as ordinary as it seems; celebrating the life of the people of Britain through the diversity which the programme finds in the activities of its own subjects/audience.

2 The world of *Nationwide* discourse 1975–7

(i) Introduction: components of the *Nationwide* discourse

The internal organisation of the *Nationwide* discourse can be represented diagramatically thus:

	Manifest content	Type of item	Dominant thematisation	Function: relation to audience
(a)	*NW* events/links	*NW* as its own subject matter	*NW* self-referential	Identification/ framing and contextualisation
(b)	World of home & leisure (i) leisure time	Magazine story-items: specifically *Nationwide* material	Stories of individuals	Entertaining, interesting, informing
	(ii) consumers		Family advice	
(c)	People's problems		Concern & care	
(d)	Image of England: town & country		Traditional values	
(e)	National/political news	'Straight' news	'Effects'/practical sense	Reporting

(ii) Description of categories

(a) *Nationwide* events/links

This section is treated first because it is these elements which, we would argue, provide the key to the organisation of the material in other sections. Two different elements are included under this heading. There are those items which have no basis 'outside' the programme and are exclusively generated by *Nationwide* itself. *Nationwide* has a wide range of self-generated items: sponsored competitions, audience- and presenter-participation events, special trips and tests which the *Nationwide* team undertake – the *Nationwide* horse, the *Nationwide* boat, Michael Barratt's farewell train around the regions, etc., etc. There are also the many places in any one programme where the *Nationwide* team provide the inter-item and inter-region links, the frames and introductions which place and position all the other items within the structure of the programme. Both elements enable the programme to establish a substantial audience-identification with the team itself; this is a basic mechanism of the programme, since the *Nationwide* team is not a team of self-effacing 'objective reporters' but are active *Nationwide* 'personalities' in their own right, and both embody and anchor the programme image. But it is also here that the critical contextualisations and evaluations are made – placing items, providing the links between items, signalling the appropriate treatments for items, giving items their 'preferred reading', towards which the audience is actively directed. This terrain of framing and contextualising is the exclusive preserve of the *Nationwide* team.

(b), (c) and (d) The world of home and leisure; people's problems; the image of England

These constitute the specific area of *Nationwide*'s concerns, which differentiate it from other areas of current affairs. Here the items tend to be inflected through a basic set of thematisations: stories of individuals, in the area of leisure; assumptions about family life, in the sphere of consumption; an orientation towards 'cause for concern' in the 'problem' section; a focus on traditional – often rural – values, in the image of England section.

There does not seem to be any simple correlation between the different areas and their particular thematisations: a 'social problem' story may be thematised through an individual, or a 'political' story through its effect on a family. The thematisations are, to some extent, flexible and variable; moreover, they may be presented in combination – a story may combine the themes of regional and individual variation. The relation of the content-areas to the various thematisations is represented in a linear form in the diagram simply to show the dominant thematisations in each particular area. These elements constitute the basis from which the *Nationwide* discourse is constituted, and, as argued, may appear in variable combinations in concrete instances.

(e) National/political news

This area, in which national issues of importance are dealt with, *Nationwide* shares with other current affairs programmes. *Nationwide*'s particularity here consists to some extent in its emphasis on 'regional news' components (e.g., 'Midlands Today'); dealing with national issues in terms of their local or regional effects, as well as purely 'local' news. As we have said, hard news material is not the staple diet of the programme – indeed it occupies a subordinate position – but it is in this area that *Nationwide*'s style of presentation approximates most to the 'straight report' format, especially in the local news slot. While the 'straight report' is the dominant form of presentation with respect to this area, it is not the only form – where possible *Nationwide* will inflect the presentation of 'the news' through its own dominant themes; that is, it will translate hard news items into stories of individuals and families. (See, for example, the stories on Meehan and the Angolan mercenaries in section (e) below.)

(iii) Analysis of categories

(a) *Nationwide* events/links

> I hope you don't mind me coming into your home in shirtsleeves. (Tom Coyne *Nationwide* 8/6/76.)

Nationwide is, above all, a friendly programme, where we're all on Christian name terms ('Over to you Bob . . .'); where we're introduced personally to new members of the *Nationwide* team and regularly given personal news about those of the team we already know. In 'serious current affairs' programming the presenter's personal life/personality does not intrude into his/her professional role. The *Nationwide* team positively exploit their different and highly developed personas – as *part of* their professional 'style' – commenting on each others' lives, hobbies, attempts to lose weight/give up smoking, etc.; portraying themselves as individuals like us, with their own problems, interests, idiosyncracies: people who know each other ('Dilys, what about you? Were you a comic freak?') and whom we can know. We get to know 'the team' as personalities – as a family, even, rather like our own: the *Nationwide* family.

The audience is constantly involved in the programme. We are invited to participate through letters, choices, ideas, etc., and our participation is acknowledged; we are asked to help (a poor family is shown on *Nationwide* 9/1/76 with not enough furniture – and our response is recorded – 100 'offers of help pour in'; 'The £ in our pockets may be shrinking, but our hearts are as big as ever'). The team give friendly advice, warnings and reminders (don't drink and drive at Xmas; remember to put your clocks on/back, etc.). The team/audience relationship is presented rather like that of the team as guests in our home, us as visitors to their studio/home.

The team is not at all stuffy, they are willing to mess about and 'have a go' – and we are entertained by their, by no means always successful, attempts to deal in unfamiliar contexts. The East Anglian boat trip on the good yacht *Nationwide* (19/5/76) is a classic example – Barratt and Wellings, two members of the national *Nationwide* team, during *Nationwide*'s week in the Norwich studio, are presented 'at sea' on a trip on the Norfolk Broads, skippered by the regional *Nationwide* presenter. The regional presenter is clearly 'at home' in this nautical context, confident and relaxed – our national presenters, though willing to try their best (Barratt gamely dressed in yachting gear, trying to get it right), cannot cope: Wellings is presented as the original landlubber, about to be seasick, unable to understand seafaring terms. He is the most sympathetic figure, standing in for our own ordinary lack of expertise; and in the end it is he who gently dismisses the specialist exercise:

> All this 'tacking' and 'avast' and 'ahoy' and left hand down and giblets and spinnakers . . . ludicrous performance.

The team are game to try, and they invite the audience to respond in like terms: viewers' competitions are a *Nationwide* speciality – 'Supersave', 'Good Neighbours', 'Citizen '76', etc. The audience are also invited to participate in the construction of the programme – 'What do you think *Nationwide*'s New Year resolution should be?' (17/12/75), and our participation becomes an item in the programme.

Audience response is scanned: we are shown on the programme both 'some of the Xmas Cards we've received from you' and also the more problem-oriented contents of the '*Nationwide* Letter Box' (29/12/75). *Nationwide* constructs an open and accessible relation to events: we watch members of the *Nationwide* team, who are presented in a self-consciously amateurish manner, participating in a *Nationwide* Showjumping Competition, set up as a parallel to the International Showjumping Competition (17/12/75); or we may see the presentation of *Nationwide* medals to Olympic athletes (15/6/76). We meet not only the 'Midlands Today puppy' (3/6/76) but also the '*Nationwide* horse' (19/5/76) – 'Realin', whose name was itself chosen by us, the *Nationwide* viewers. Val introduces us to the horse, points out how we may recognise it in a race, and explains the factors relevant to racing success. Here we are invited to participate (as surrogate 'horse-owners') in 'the sport of kings' – an area from which as normal individuals we would be excluded – through the mediation of the *Nationwide* team.

Links and mediations

At many points the *Nationwide* discourse becomes self-referential – *Nationwide* and the *Nationwide* team are not only the mediators who bring the stories to us, but themselves become the subject of the story. This is the 'maximal' development of one consistent thread in the programme – the attempt to establish a close, personalised relationship between the *Nationwide* team and the audience. A 'mystery item' (on *Nationwide* 28/9/76) turns out to be *Nationwide*'s own 'tele-test' with an invited audience who submit themselves to the process of research into their comprehension of *Nationwide* items. Here we have invited 'experts' whose views are elicited; but they are subordinated to the direct relation between *Nationwide* and its audience: it is principally a 'participation' item: we see *Nationwide* in reflection on itself, in dialogue with its own audience.

However, this aspect of the *Nationwide* discourse is not sustained only through the manifest content of those odd items where *Nationwide* and its audience have become the subject of its own story – it is also sustained through the 'links' between any and every item in a programme. Here the team appear in their capacity as links/mediators – getting out there 'on the spot', bringing us the variety, topical stories, drama of life in Britain today: bringing the regions to each other and to the centre, the parts to the whole. It is the team who must construct a world of shared attitudes and expectations between us all in order to hold the heterogeneous elements of *Nationwide* together.

Links can be made in various ways – through familiar presenters' faces in the studio, through the extraction of some element from the last item ('it may not be the weather for . . .') linked to an extracted element from the next item ('but it's certainly the right day for . . .'), through the establishing of shared ground between commentator and viewer. The central components of these links tend to be references to a level of shared attitudes towards the taken-for-granted world: concern about the weather, holidays, anxiety at rising prices/taxes, exasperation with bureaucracy.

The audience is constantly implicated through the linkperson's discourse, by the use of personal pronouns: 'tonight we meet . . .', 'we all of us know that . . .', '. . . can happen to any of us', 'so we asked . . .'. The audience is also implicated by reference to past or coming items, which we have all seen/will see, and (by implication) all interpret in the same way. There is a reiterated assertion of a co-temporality ('nowadays', 'in these times of . . .') which through its continuous present/immediacy transcends the differences between us: 'of course . . .' *Nationwide* assumes we all live in the same social world.

The relations between the team and the viewers are constantly mystified in the discourse of *Nationwide*. There is no credit sequence at the end or beginning of the programme; without reference to the *Radio Times*, we can only know them informally and internally, as they refer to each other, people who know each other, so that we too know them like that, like people we already know rather than as presenters/TV personnel. (In their absence, people on the programme are referred to by their full names – 'A report from Luke Casey in Leighton Heath', in the more formal manner of an introduction, but in general these are precisely not the core team.) This already-knowingness, the *Nationwide* team in our living rooms as friends, constantly catches us with them as 'we', in their world, which purports to be nothing more than a reflection of our world.

This can be most clearly seen in the use (*Nationwide* 19/5/76) of 'Let's . . .'. Tom Coyne: 'Let's take a look at our weather picture'; 'Let's go to Norwich'; Michael Barratt: 'Let's hear from another part of East Anglia.' Here, the audience's real separation from the team is represented in the form of a unity or community of interests between team and audience; the construction of this imaginary community appears as a proposition we can't refuse – we are made equal partners in the *Nationwide* venture, while simultaneously our autonomy is denied. This, with its attendant possessive, '*our* weather picture', is the least ambiguous form of the 'co-optive we', which is a major feature of the discourse and linking strategies in *Nationwide*.

Links discourse sometimes seems to be structured in the recognition of the different positions of presenters and audience. Michael Barratt: 'And after *your own* programmes *we* go cruising down the river to bring *you our* third programme from East Anglia.' (Nation/region link.) But this difference is also constantly elided and recuperated:

(1) By reference to a wider, shared context or frame, in which we are all 'we' together: a context which embraces us all, establishing a false equivalence/homogeneity between us, dismantling our real differences of position and power. Here, through this construction, they unashamedly establish us in position in the discourse in a place which enables them to 'speak for us'. For example (19/5/76):

Tomorrow we'll have some sunny intervals . . .

If our society was destroyed, heaven forbid . . .

(2) Through the denial of the inequality of the audience/presenter relation-

ship. Although the form of this relationship is friendly and familiar – conducive to we-ness – it is actually only *they* who can speak and initiate action. Thus, when Michael Barratt says 'so we thought that tonight we'd go racing', although he may strictly be referring only to the studio group, 'we the audience' are implicated because if they go racing, we go racing, unless we switch channels.

This elision, this constant concealing of the one-way nature of the television system in our society, their negotiation of the isolation of their medium, lays the basis for a whole set of ways in which the *Nationwide* audience is implicated in, and identifies with, 'the scene *Nationwide*' (15/6/76).

Identification is also produced and reinforced through the chatty informality of the links. The links themselves are signified as transparent – bearing no substantial meaning of their own, made only of the reference to past or coming items. However, as already discussed, they also signify 'we-ness', which is constantly constructed by both the team and the viewing subject to mean 'nationwideness'. The seemingly neutral links themselves, always carrying this 'other', extra meaning, the 'being-among-friends in one's living room', are constantly contributing to the construction of the meaning of *Nationwide*, which we are always already implicated in, because it is with us, the viewers, that this assumption of intimacy is made.

This can perhaps be seen more clearly, in a slightly more developed form, in *Nationwide*'s presentation of the weather forecast. The weather forecast on BBC television generally takes the standard form of a map of the British Isles, with graphic devices and a commentary over. On 'Midlands Today', the Midlands regional component of *Nationwide*, this standard signifier is replaced by a child's painting, usually showing fairly extreme climatic conditions, with a voice-over commentary. The new signifier is recognised in two ways. The artist's name and age are given, and the linkperson usually makes some comment about the 'content' of the picture, or about the weather at that point:

Tom Coyne: Well with the drizzle coming down, I hardly dare mention it, but let's take a look at our weather picture. (*Nationwide* 19/5/76.)

What happens here is that the painting, as well as signifying 'weather', also signifies 'children send paintings in to *Nationwide*'. The signifier is emptied of its own meaning (man with umbrella), to mean 'weather' *and* resignified, in the meta-language of the programme's own discourse on itself, as: 'this is a programme which children send in pictures to' – *Nationwide* is our programme. (For a similar point in relation to advertisements, see Williamson 1978.)

The most elaborate form of this process comes when this 'nationwideness' bursts out of the links and generates its own items, which we have called *Nationwide* events, which don't require reference to the outside world at all, only to the *Nationwide* 'we'. A great deal of the strategic work of the *Nationwide* discourse consists of operations around the construction of this

Nationwide 'we'. It would be wrong to present these as yielding a fixed and unproblematic structure of positions. In fact, it would be more correct to see the programme as struggling to constitute this set of equivalences around the shifting pronouns – we/us, negotiating this divergence/unity, constantly attempting to secure an identity between these two terms of its speech: an identity it aims for, but cannot guarantee.

Both Roman Jakobson and Roland Barthes have pointed to the critical position of the personal pronouns in discourse, as the location of what Jakobson calls 'duplex structures'. Personal pronouns are *shifters*, in the sense that if, in conversation, A speaks to B in terms of 'I' and 'you', B can only reply coherently by transposing or 'shifting' the terms: A's 'I' and 'you' become B's 'you' and 'I'. Jakobson calls 'shifters' terms of transference, the site of a critical overlapping and circularity in discourse, which thus, through the ambiguity of the 'double structure' of language, can become, at the level of the code, the site of complex ideological work. The shifting of the pronouns of the enunciation and what is enunciated – based on a rule of conversation (c.f., Barthes 1967) – becomes the potential space for the exploitation of an ideological ambiguity which can serve to construct new positions for 'speaker' and 'audience' in relation to the discourse employed. What *Nationwide* seems to represent is not a secured correspondence between speaker and hearer positions such as could sustain an unproblematic equivalence between them – for this would be manifestly an 'imaginary' equivalence in a discourse dominated by the originating practices of the *Nationwide* team, and the structured 'absence' of the audience (the latter may be represented as the imaginary enunciator of *Nationwide*'s speech but in the real relations of TV communication it can only-always be the object of the enunciation). What we find, instead, are multiple strategies designed to secure this 'correspondence' of positions – strategies which seek to exploit the terms of transference; and this results, in the actual discourse of particular programmes, in an unstable fluctuation around and through this double structure:

Tonight we meet . . . and then we join . . . that's us at six . . . After your own programme we go cruising. We also meet . . . and we consider . . . Our own horse is looking good . . . and we ask . . . What's to be done about it *Nationwide*. (19/5/76.)

The mechanisms for the construction of the 'co-optive we' depend on and are realised in language: but they do not operate exclusively at the level of language in the narrow sense. In *Nationwide*, we suggest, they are further secured by and through the 'positioning' of the team – the presenters who represent and 'personify' the programme. And this is a feature, not of *Nationwide* alone (where, however, it is a prominent and characteristic presence) but in the discourses of 'popular TV' more generally. The *Radio Times* observed long ago about *Tonight*, the programme which has a key position in setting the terms and establishing the traditions which structure the practice of 'popular TV':

the items [were] knitted together into a continuous and comprehensive show by a personality, starting off with Cliff Michelmore . . . (*Radio Times* 26/8/60.)

The *Nationwide* presenters attempt to identify as closely as possible with 'you, the viewers'. The team speak on our behalf, mediating the world to us; they assume a position as our representatives. Lord Hill noted, of *Tonight* (but the observation could easily be extended to *Nationwide*), that the first essential of a reporter is:

not unselfconsciousness or camera presence, but a total conviction that he represents the absolute norm, and that any deviation from his way of life is suspect. (Quoted in Connell 1975.)

The team are not stars in the sense of telepersonalities but:

real people; whole rounded people who ask the sort of questions that are sound common-sense – questions that are in the viewers' mind and that he would ask if he was in their place. (Quoted in Connell 1975.)

Thus, the relationships which are established between programme and audience, which set the viewer in place in a certain relation to the discourse – here, a relation of identity and complicity – are sustained in the mechanisms and strategies of the discourses of popular television themselves, but also by the presenters, who have a key role in anchoring those positions and in impersonating – personifying – them. The linking/framing discourse, then, which plays so prominent a part in structuring any sequence of items in *Nationwide*, and guides us between the variety of heterogeneous contents which constitute *Nationwide* as a unity-in-variety, not only informs us about what the next item is, and maintains the 'naturalism' of smooth flow and easy transitions – bridging, binding, linking items into *a* programme. It also re-positions 'us' into – inside – the speech of the programme itself, and sets us up in a particular position of 'knowledge' to the programme by (also) positioning us with 'the team'; implicating 'us' in what the team knows, what it assumes, in the team's relationships with each other, and the team's relation to 'that other, vital part of *Nationwide*' – us, the audience. For, as the (one-time) editor Michael Bunce put it, it is not only Michael Barratt, or the *Nationwide* team, who decide what goes on the air, so does the audience:

Telephone calls, telegrams, 1000 letters a week . . . breathe life into the programme and inspire much of what actually gets on the air . . . [the presenters] do not make *Nationwide*. The viewers make it. (Quoted in Gillman 1975.)

Identification and preferred readings

However, while our participation as audience may be necessary to the programme, 'we' do not make it in a relationship of equivalence with the 'team'. It is the team who control and define the terms of the discourse, and it is the team who signal to us 'what it's all about'. It is the presenters who 'explain' the very meaning of the images we see on the screen. The 'menu' for the 19/5/76 item on the students:

> Tonight we meet the students who built a new life for themselves out of a load of old rubbish. These may look like a few old plastic bags to you, but actually, for a time it was home to them.

positions viewer, *Nationwide* team and interviewees within a paradox of the programme's own construction.

It is 'we' together who will meet the students, but it is the *Nationwide* team who will offer a privileged reading of the actual significance of the images on the screen, which the audience at home is thus caught into 'reading' as 'a few old plastic bags'. This systematic subversion of the 'obvious' reading an audience might have made of an image, apart from the implications it has for the constantly set-up 'natural' and shared decoding, renders the audience rationally impotent, because the conditions of the paradox are always that it is impossible to know what the image really denotes. The consequent dependence of the audience on the broadcasters' explanation of each little mystery accentuates, in a self-justifying way, the team's role as our 'representatives'.

The presenters and interviewers define for us the status of the extra-programme participants and their views: through these introductions, links and frames the preferred readings or contextualisations of the items and events portrayed are suggested. In the 19/5/76 programme, for instance, we are 'directed' by Tom Coyne's gruff, fair, but 'no-nonsense' manner towards a rather low estimation of the activities of the students who 'built a new life for themselves out of a load of old rubbish'. After all, they cannot compete with the basically 'sensible' perspective expressed in Coyne's final, indulgently-phrased question:

> Now I can obviously see that a student of your age is going to enjoy an experience like this, even if the weather is rough, because it's a lot of fun, but other people want to know what you actually got out of it from an educational point of view . . .?

Moreover, here Coyne not only invokes our views on the matter but implicates us in his. He does not merely ask a common-sense question, but claims to do so on behalf of us; we are the viewers – those 'other people' who 'want to know'.

(b) The world of home and leisure

Let us begin with an analogy between 'the scene *Nationwide*' and Duckburg:— Dorfman and Mattelart observe of Duckburg:

> In the world of Disney, no one has to work to produce. There is a constant round of buying, selling and consuming, but to all appearances none of the products involved has required any effort whatsoever to make ... The process of production has been eliminated but the products remain. What for? To be consumed. Of the capitalist process which goes from production to consumption, Disney knows only the second stage ... (Dorfman and Mattelart 1975, pp. 64–5.)

Foremost among the areas of life from which *Nationwide* draws its material is the world of 'leisure' – the sphere of culture, entertainments and hobbies. Here we meet individuals in their personal capacities, away from the world of social production; we follow their activities in the realms of their personal life. The nation '*Nationwide*', like the inhabitants of Duckburg, seems to be principally concerned with the process of consumption. Unlike Duckburg though, we consume principally in families – entering the Supersave competition (Monday nights 1975) together, and even enlarging our family size together ('Citizen 76' Monday nights 1976).

The world of home and leisure is by far the dominant single element in the *Nationwide* discourse, accounting for 40% of the items in the sample (see figures at the end of this chapter). The first thing to remark is that this 'presence' betokens the almost total absence (except in some local news items) of the world of work, the struggle of and over production. This private leisure-world is a 'free floating' sphere from which the productive base has been excised. This absence extends to production in the family. Although 'Citizen 76' focused on pregnancy and the birth of children, and at Christmas we have shared selected hostesses' Christmas menus ('Christmas Round the World' 1975), the day-to-day labour of childcare and housework, which makes the home a sphere of work and not leisure to most women, is invisible in *Nationwide*. *Nationwide* leaves us suspended in the seemingly autonomous spheres of circulation, consumption and exchange: the real relations of productive life, both inside and outside the home, have vanished.

Nationwide addresses itself (cf., *Radio Times* billing) to an audience of individuals and families, the nation, in their personal capacities. Its transmission time allows it to construct itself/constructs it at the bridging point between 'work' and home (for wage workers). Its discourse is structured through the absent/present opposition between the 'world' and home. This opposition between the public and the private, we would argue, is partly informed by the sexual division associated with 'world' and 'home' (Rowbotham 1973). It is the 'masculine' world of work which constructs the home as a place of leisure, a private sphere where the male labourer has some sort of choice and control, which exists quite differently for women (who may well also be wage workers), as it is their responsibility to maintain this 'tent pitched in a world not right'.

As a family show, *Nationwide* addresses itself to the family together, 'caring and sharing' (Thompson 1977), a close knit group of individuals, among whom the 'obviousness' of the sexual division of labour emerges as simply different responsibilities, specialities and qualities for men and women. Thus *Nationwide* does not, like women's magazines, address itself primarily to the 'woman's world' of the home, with advice about 'coping' and 'managing' which reveal the contradictory tension of maintaining the 'ideal' 'norm' (Winship 1978). *Nationwide* doesn't have recipes, dress and knitting patterns or household hints, unless there's something special about them: a man who makes his children's clothes ('Supersave'); if we slim, we slim together, *Nationwide* ('Slim and Trim' March 1977, with *Nationwide*'s 'ten guinea-pig slimmers' – *Radio Times* 30/3/77). We meet the family together, usually in their home ('Supersave', 'Citizen 76', 'Budget' 1977), or its individuals in relation to their own speciality. Sometimes, for women, this is 'being a wife and mother', as in the interview with the Pfleigers in the 'Little Old England' item 19/5/77, which opens with a shot of Mrs. Pfleiger at the kitchen sink, and is cut so that her answer to the question 'Did you find it difficult to settle in here?' is entirely concerned with household equipment, while her husband gives a more general account of the family's history and attitudes. More usually it is being a wife and mother *and also* being fascinated by lions (19/4/77), being a witch (18/6/76), making a tapestry of Bristol's history (15/6/76).

We are concerned, then, with a discourse which, very schematically, and at a general level, has an underlying 'preferred' structure of absences and presences:

ABSENT	:	PRESENT
world		home
work		leisure
production ⎱ reproduction ⎰		consumption
workers (functions)		individuals (bearers)
structural causation		effects

There is a concentration on 'the "real" world of people' (Hoggart 1957) both as a bulwark against the abstract, alien problems of the outside world, and as a moral baseline through which they are interrogated. The effectivity of the outside world is symbolised for *Nationwide* in 'bureaucracy' – faceless men (non-individuals, but still personalised to the extent that it is 'faceless men', not 'the system'), behind closed doors, who have power over 'us':

Once again, the key decisions were taken behind closed doors, in this case the small branch meetings up and down the country. (*Nationwide* 15/6/76.)

25

In relation to these issues *Nationwide* will adopt a 'campaigning' stance – aiming to 'open doors' on our behalf. Thus in Autumn '76 we had the creation of 'Public Eye': a spot in which two team members

> investigate an issue which they feel should be brought under the gaze of the public eye. (*Radio Times* 3/11/76.)

This opposition between we 'ordinary people' and the 'faceless men' of the bureaucracy is close in structure to Hoggart's description of a class sense of 'them' and 'us':

> Towards 'Them' generally, as towards the police, the primary attitude is not so much fear as mistrust; mistrust accompanied by a lack of illusions about what 'They' will do for one, and the complicated way – the apparently unnecessarily complicated way – in which 'They' order one's life when it touches them. (Hoggart 1957, p. 74.)

The difference is that the 'us' *Nationwide* speaks for is not class specific, but 'the nation' of consuming individuals, always already in families. In the example above, the decisions taken 'behind closed doors' were made by workers in Trade Union branches. (Cf., Morley 1976, section 1.b, on presentation of TU decisions as the sole cause of events.)

Classes do not appear in the discourse of *Nationwide*; only individuals, and these individuals usually appear in relation to the market – in the spheres of exchange and consumption. Thus the image of a group of white male workers with clenched fists standing outside a factory gate (*Nationwide* 19/5/76) is *not* an image of workers victorious in a struggle at the point of production, but that of a group of Pools winners:

> altogether nine people will share the prize money, and for one of the winner's wives, news of the win came as an unexpected but most welcome 44th birthday present. (19/5/76.)

This is not to suggest that *Nationwide* does not, or can never, deal with the worlds of production and hard news, but that when confronted with the need to cover political items, such as the budget or incomes policies, *Nationwide* deals with them where possible by translating them into the context of domestic life; how will such 'political' issues affect the home. The strategy is precisely that of the humanisation/personalisation of 'issues' into their 'effects on people'; or, alternatively, the exploration of the range of people's 'feelings' or reactions to external forces that impinge on them. (For example, the new tax schedule: 'Do you recognise that – one of those nasty PAYE forms . . . an all time grouse . . . along with mothers-in-law' – *Nationwide* 29/3/77.)

Political events then in this discourse have their meaning made comprehensible through their *effects* on 'people', and it is assumed that people are normally grouped in families:

> We ... look at how this budget affects three typical families ... 'Ken' feels strongly he's not getting a fair deal at the moment ... what would you like to see the Chancellor doing for your family and friends? ... (*Nationwide* 29/3/77.)

Nationwide asks 'home' questions in the world. If we enter into that larger domain, it is to find out what the people in the public world are like – as individuals; for example, that an MP is also a racehorse owner (19/5/76). The structures of ownership and control in society are dissolved into the huge variety of individuals *Nationwide* – it takes all sorts to make a world. Where this type of treatment is not possible, it is because some crisis in that world has made its day-to-day absence no longer tenable in the programme discourse; its effects, at this point, intrude into the concerns of the *Nationwide* World – which at some level involves a recognition of the determinacy of this outside world. But this is precisely registered as intrusion, interruption or inconvenience. (Cf., Morley 1976, section 5b on the reporting of strikes as a regrettable disruption of 'normal working'.)

The world of home and leisure, then, is the primary space of *Nationwide*'s concerns. Within this overall field we can differentiate between (b.i) – items drawn from leisure time activities – and (b.ii) – items dealing with consumers and domesticity. The former is the space of 'free time' and individual pursuits, the latter is the largely unstated premise of the *Nationwide* discourse – the predication of the nuclear family as the basic unit of social organisation.

(i) leisure time

Items drawn from the 'world of leisure' account for almost 25% ($\frac{40}{182}$) of the items in the sample. Moreover, within these items it is individuals, pursuing their different hobbies and leisure interests (this stress on difference precisely connoting their individuality), who are the principal subjects of the *Nationwide* discourse. Of the 40 items in this category 50% are thematised around the 'story of an individual' ('Tonight we meet the man who ...'): from the story (9/1/76) of the owner of a card-playing parrot to that of the creator of a strip cartoon of the life of Jesus Christ (17/8/76), or even (*Nationwide* 22/1/76) the story of a man who:

> made a fortune because he has a child-like obsession for a toy – we fly a kite with a difference high above the Cotswolds.

This last too is a 'success' story with a 'difference'; the story of 'a simple man' with a 'child-like obsession' – and a bonus: a kite with a difference, which has been bought by a Japanese business man with a keen eye for 'making a yen'.

27

Barratt: Whenever/we/can in *Nationwide*/we/try to bring you/the bright
side of life to counter all the gloom and the despondency around/us./
And tonight we have a success story for you about a Cotswolds man
who's turned a childhood delight into a booming business. James Hogg
went to meet him . . .
Hogg: Unbelievable. And if I tell you that Peter Powell has just received
a tax demand for £83,000 after one year, you'll get some measure of his
outstanding and astounding personal success.

The peculiarly important role of these 'personal' stories is that, despite
their particularity, they function principally as counterpoints to 'the normal':
the story above infers the normal at the same time as it demonstrates the
possibilities of individual 'transcendence' – success = the lucky personal
break; but, 'it could happen to anyone'. The little structure represented by
this item is worth analysing. It invokes something normal – a 'lowest common
denominator': Peter Powell, like the rest of us, is not a 'special person' in the
sense of having status or power in the public world. However, this does not
submerge him into the invisible average, for that 'ordinariness' depends, in
fact, on 'the difference' – something which makes him 'individual and
particular', within his ordinariness. What, indeed, is average and normal
about everyone is that each person is different, in his or her unique
individuality. And this 'difference' opens the possibility – which can,
hypothetically, befall anyone – that an ordinary hobby can become the basis
of a raging success story. But even this extraordinary 'turn of events' or
'twist of fate' is coupled back or recuperated for the norm; one person's
hobby is presented, not simply in its unique individuality, but as one more
example – in a litany of examples – of the extraordinary variety of interesting
hobbies that *all* we ordinary people (the audience) have, 'Nationwide'.
    This means that items often spotlight one aspect of an 'otherwise ordinary'
person's life. *Nationwide* discovers that 'behind' what seems ordinary/normal
there is variety and difference. The point is, as Bunce, the programme's ex-
editor, put it

We want to show that individuality hasn't been stamped out. We are
not all grey, drab people. (Quoted in Gillman 1975.)

On *Nationwide* 29/12/75 we meet Miss Evelyn Dainty, who looks just like
everybody's Granny; she turns out, in fact, to be exactly that – everybody's
Granny. What's special about Miss Dainty is that she's 'adopted 250 kids
throughout the world' and she sends every one of them a card at Christmas.
She spends 'everything she earns on Christmas cards'. 'This selfless charity
has become' – *Nationwide* assures us – 'a complete way of life . . . simple,
hardworking and at first sight, very solitary'.
    This is in fact a favoured *Nationwide* style of presentation; a narrative
technique is used – the item is a 'little story' – and the 'angle' is 'what is it that
this place/person which/who looks normal is going to turn out to be/do?'

These *Nationwide* stories create a spurious impression of 'investigative journalism' (which informs the reporters' roles); but an investigative journalism that concerns itself with People, not issues – the reporters go out into the world only to discover – reconfirm the existence of – this 'variety in ordinariness'.

One category of individuals for whom there is a special place in the *Nationwide* discourse is precisely that of 'eccentrics' – people so obsessed by their 'specialisms' as to be extra-normal: whether the mildly troublesome 'hermit of the Cotswolds who doesn't want any friends' (1/6/76) or the men who play at World War II in miniature tanks in the woods (30/12/75). But eccentricity itself easily slides into being an 'achievement'; when we meet 'the man who served yakburgers on the roof of the world' (11/6/76: a mountaineering cook) we are interested in him as much for the eccentricity of what he did when he got there as for his achievement in climbing the mountain.

The extreme example of eccentricity was represented by the (1/6/76) multimillionaire who tired of business and social intercourse, and bought Tony Jacklin's old house and retired there, virtually without friends or contacts, save for the occasional visit of a head gardener; who spends his time indulging bizarre whims, like jumping each day fully clothed into his swimming pool, or feeding model cars to the fire. This item is given the full Gothic Horror Movie treatment by James Hogg (reporting), complete with unsteady camera making its own way up the overgrown path to the Hammer-style front door, to the sound of barking Baskerville hounds off-stage and the strains of the only record which Mr. David keeps permanently on the hi-fi. This truly extra-ordinary, upper-class eccentric – 'the most reclusive multimillionaire since Howard Hughes' – has really so entirely abandoned the land of the ordinary that there is nothing whatsoever left to connect him to us except his eccentricity – a category which, however, in the pantheon of English traditionalism, has, paradoxically, its own 'normal-abnormal' space reserved; indeed, oversubscribed. But he must pay the penalty for his waywardness from the norm. He is – as *Nationwide* itself moralises – the 'rich man who [quite abnormally] doesn't want friends.'

We are concerned, however, with 'serious' individual achievements as well. When *Nationwide* covered the New Years Honours List (2/1/76) it featured precisely not the already famous, but those ordinary members of the public working quietly away at their tasks (a man knighted for fifty years work in land drainage; a cleaner) whose more mundane achievements had been honoured – ordinary people as 'stars' in their ordinary activities.

News values of a more usual kind reassert themselves from time to time. *Nationwide* specialises in discovering and presenting the really extraordinary achievements of particular individuals. We meet not only the blind person who 'watches' tennis (18/6/76), and the 70 year old part-time art student sculptress: 'I thought I'd have a go . . .'/'My gosh, they're good . . . It's never too late to learn . . . I wonder how many people have got talent like that . . .' (30/3/77), but also 'Mrs. D. Louise Dingwall' an '89 year old female racehorse trainer' in a 'tough and masculine world' (29/12/75). Here the value of achievements has a particular resonance: they are individuals who have overcome the handicaps of disability, old age and sex in their chosen spheres of activity.

(ii) consumers and domesticity

Items on domestic life and 'consumers' problems' are the fourth most prominent theme in the sample, accounting for 17% ($\frac{33}{182}$) of the sample. As noted, the material in this category alone exceeds the space given to national political items (15%), and in combination with the other 'natural' elements of the *Nationwide* discourse these kinds of items overshadow the 'serious current affairs' material by a substantial margin.

Family life at times appears directly as an area of concern for *Nationwide* – when threatened for instance by 'politics'; e.g., housing policies which may 'cause families to be split up' (13/2/74), but also as a cause for celebration. The Christmas 1975 sample is rife with material of this kind, from 'Wilfred Pickles' family Christmas' (19/12/75) – 'Christmas is also a time for families . . .' – to the more down to earth, practically oriented 'food from Christmas leftovers', and even 'remedies for too much Christmas food' (29/12/75).

The predication of *Nationwide*'s discourse on the centrality of the nuclear family emerged most clearly in an item ('Midlands Today' 23/11/76) on some demographic research which showed that 'more married couples each year are deciding to have no children'. The introduction clearly identified the threat posed to the family as we know it.

Introduction, over family-at-home snapshot: 'A typical family snapshot picture of mum and dad there, surrounded by their happy children, could fade from view the way the population figures are dropping these days.'

The item went on to interview the researchers at some length, itself an indication of the weight *Nationwide* attributed to this problem, given the noticeable absence of any concern with the results of academic research in 'normal' *Nationwide* discourse. Indeed the 'relevance' of this research had to be clearly marked out as having general social value:

You're carrying out this research. Now why? What's the information going to do for us?

The failure to conform to the nuclear pattern was posed as an explicit and threatening problem:

Now you yourself are married without children . . . why have you decided not to have them?

. . . is it a selfish attitude not to produce that child?

30

These questions were all premised against a set of equations between

children = women's work
parents = married couples
families = marriages
birthrate = births to married couples.

which surfaced perhaps most clearly in a slip of the tongue by the interviewer, when he addressed the researchers:

. . . as parents yourselves without children . . .

Expectations about the nuclear family structure the dialogue so thoroughly that it is impossible, here, for the interviewer even to speak clearly about the breakdown of these norms: the aberration leads only to an uncomfòrtable blurring of categories.

The dominant tendency in the material in this area, which has made categorisation particularly difficult (see Appendix: Notes on Categorisation) is for the form of the family to be assumed as the baseline experience of the audience. 'The family' is often not so much explicitly present in the discourse, as it is precisely an unspecified premise or 'absence' on which the discourse is predicated. Thus *Nationwide*'s 'Supersave' competition had as its competitors not individuals, but families: families who competed to live most economically in these dire times, succeeding through feats like making cot sheets, aprons and an evening skirt out of a double sheet. The families up and down the country were tested in the realms of cooking, shopping, do-it-yourself and money management; and the super-domestic winners were rewarded with four minutes 'free shopping' in a supermarket which we, the ordinarily domestic audience, were able to watch on speeded up film (2/1/76).

Primarily, then, the items assume the existence of the audience already, and necessarily, structured into nuclear family groupings. The discourse adopts a stance of giving 'practical advice' in relation to the problems of consumption experienced by families – this way of thematising the material is the dominant one in this area, accounting for nearly half $(\frac{16}{33})$ of the items in this category.

The material that is thematised in this way can be quite diverse – from topical items: 'Grow your own vegetables to beat drought prices'/'Travel to wet places for your holidays' (18/8/76) to issues of perennial concern to us all: 'The need for a will' (6/1/76) or advice to viewers on 'insurance problems' (5/1/76). *Nationwide* here, of course, attempts to be up with our current concerns, able to bring us a timely fog warning from the 'Traffic Unit' (15/12/75) as well as advice on the advantages of laminated windscreens from the 'Consumer Unit' (17/12/75) – a subject on which *Nationwide* had orchestrated a consumer/viewer's campaign against an unresponsive government bureaucracy in the Department of the Environment.

Nationwide thus establishes a predominantly practical relation with the

31

domestic audience – offering advice and warnings on subjects as diverse as the dangerous materials used in some toy pandas (9/1/76) and the necessity of insuring your house against possible subsidence (18/8/76) or storm damage (5/1/76). We must all deal with the changing state of the law where this intrudes into our lives – here again *Nationwide* can help, offering advice on how to deal with the breathalyser, TV licence laws (18/12/75) and the sex discimination laws (29/12/75 and 9/1/76).

Nationwide is also concerned to play a campaigning/defensive role, protecting the interests of us all as consumers, not only against the abuse of power by monopolistic 'big unions', but also against the inefficiency of state bureaucracies. In a report on a 'price increase coming from the gas board' (31/3/71), the angle was clearly stated in the introductory framing statement: 'What concerns us is that it may be a needless increase' – *Nationwide* here clearly has the viewers' best interests at heart. An interview with the relevant expert then probes the 'necessity' for the increase and points to the hardship it may cause. This meets with a frosty response, and all Michael Barratt can say in conclusion, after trying his best on our behalf, is

So, pay up and try to smile about it.

The centrality of this theme in the programme discourse is also evidenced by the whole role of the 'Consumer Unit' in the development of *Nationwide*. This was the first area where *Nationwide* set up a specialist/regular slot in the programme to deal in 'investigative journalism' in a consistent way. (Cf., Gillman 1975.)

(c) People's problems

Nationwide is a 'responsible' programme; it will not only amuse and interest us. *Nationwide* is a programme of care and concern and consistently runs stories on 'people's problems': the problems of the lonely, the abnormal, underprivileged and (especially the physically) disabled. These items account for the third largest part of the sample: 16% ($\frac{30}{182}$). The point here is that *Nationwide* deals with these stories in a quite distinctive way; rather than the discussion between experts that we might get on *Panorama* about the background to some 'social problem' *Nationwide* takes us straight to the 'human effects' – the problems and feelings of the 'sufferers', what effect their disability has 'on their everyday lives'.

Nationwide seems to have a penchant for dealing with cases of physical abnormality: where the 'problem' is seen to have natural, not social origins – blindness, handicaps, etc. The angle they take is usually a 'positive' one: 'look what is being done for these people with new technology'. The social role of technology – of inventions and inventors – is stressed here; useful technology is seen to solve social problems by demonstrably improving the quality of people's lives. This is indicative of *Nationwide*'s concern with 'human scale technology' in 'Britain Today', where, as Tom Coyne says (19/5/76), 'Things are changing all the time' – it is the world of 'new developments', such as an invention which enables blind students to produce 3-dimensional drawings (19/5/76).

Physical abnormality, without its social origins or consequences, is very much part of that 'natural human' world on which *Nationwide* frequently reports, and from which it regularly draws its stock of internally-generated reporters' 'stories'. A London region item on the treatment of a thalidomide child, for example, made no reference to the origins of the case, the contentious question of compensation, or the degree of the drug company's responsibility, or the suppression of the *Sunday Times* report. It was concerned, precisely, with finding the means to normalise the life of those affected by thalidomide without reference to the more troublesome question of causes.

The destruction of nature and the effect of natural disability recur again and again: 'Threat to rare birds by egg collectors' (29/3/77); 'Cause for Concern: Christmas pets' (15/12/75); 'Cause for Concern: rare animals' (2/1/76); the problems of 'Hay Fever Sufferers' (9/6/76); the problem of 're-employment of the blind' (3/6/76). But *Nationwide* is also concerned with other kinds of social misfits for whom something must be done. The problems are 'brought home' to us, and in these areas of 'ordinary human concern', *Nationwide* wears its heart on its sleeve: we see the problem, but we are also shown the positive side – what can be done about it.

Thus we learn of the anguish caused to relatives by 'disappearing people' (1/6/76) but we also meet 'Brigadier Grettin', from a voluntary organisation, who 'devotes his life to trying to find missing people'. We hear of 'old people alone at Christmas' (19/12/75), but also of positive responses: 'six men riding a bike for charity' (19/8/76), people collecting waste, and 'marathon singers' performing for charitable funds (17/6/76).

Nationwide monitors, on our behalf, serious and topical issues – thus not only are there the occasional, 'investigative', reports on the problems of soccer violence (20/1/76) and West Indian children's educational problems (30/3/77), but also responses to 'topical' issues directly affecting us all. So, during the rabies scare, *Nationwide* featured 'rabies remedies' (11/6/76); during the drought, not only an investigation of 'whose responsibility' its problems were (20/8/76), but also practical warnings of 'cuts in our areas' (17/8/76) and of 'diseases from the drought' (20/8/76).

Nationwide's treatment of people's problems is then, immediate: we are shown 'what it means in human terms'. This 'humanising' emphasis can be seen to have its basis in the specific communicative strategy of the broadcasters – in trying to 'get the issue across' what better way than to concentrate directly on the feelings of those immediately involved? However, the consequent emphasis, being placed almost exclusively on this 'human angle', serves to inflect our awareness of the issue; what is rendered invisible by this style of presentation is the relation of these human problems to the structure of society. The stress on 'immediate effects', on 'people', on getting to the heart of the problem, paradoxically confines *Nationwide* rigidly to the level of 'mere appearances'.

The *Nationwide* discourse in this area is in fact structured by two dimensions of the same 'significant absence'. On the one hand the problems that are dealt with are almost exclusively those with a natural, not social, origin – especially problems arising from physical disability. Here the 'problems' generated by the class structure of our society are largely evaded, through the tendency to naturalise social problems. On the other hand the treatment of these problems consistently evades the social determinations acting on the experience of physical problems: thus the items on people suffering from physical disability do not address themselves to the differential class experience of these problems.

The social dimensions of the problem are consistently excised – they are constantly re-presented as the problems of particular individuals, deprived of their social context. Moreover the horizon of the problem is set in terms of what can be done about it immediately – by charitable work, by individual voluntary effort, or by 'new technology'. The systematic displacement of the discourse to the level of individual effort makes logical, as one of its consequences, this stress on practical, pragmatic remedies. This is not to deny the importance of these matters, but to point to the absence of any awareness of the need for social and structural solutions to structurally generated problems.

We would suggest that in a parallel fashion to the way in which class structure is largely invisible in the *Nationwide* 'image of England' (see section (d) and conclusion) – and is only presented through the displaced form of 'regional differences' – in this area of *Nationwide* discourse 'natural disabilities' stand as a similarly displaced 'representation' of the absent level of socially generated inequalities and problems.

(d) The image of England: town and country

The discourse of *Nationwide* takes as a matter of explicit concern and value our national cultural heritage; the category accounts for 15% ($\frac{31}{182}$) of the sample.

The 'culture' in which *Nationwide* deals is of course the cultural heritage of 'middle Britain'; it is decidedly not the up-to-the-minute culture of the pop world (the Sex Pistols made their breakthrough on *Today*, not *Nationwide*) nor the world of 'high culture'. It's the world of the 'Cook Family Circus' (18/6/76) and the anniversary of '30 years since the last ENSA show' (20/8/76). Reunion and anniversary are a recurring thread in the items; it may equally well be 'Pilots in pre-war planes reliving Biggles' (17/8/76), or 'Dakota planes 40 years old today' (17/12/75), or even a Burma P.O.W. reunion (9/1/76). The cultural context is neither the Rainbow nor Covent Garden: it is rather Blackpool (3/3/76) or 'holidays in Spain' (1/6/76). The cultural context is often constructed through the mass of calendar items which punctuate the *Nationwide* year: from the Glorious 12th, to Hallowe'en, Christmas, Ascot, St. George's Day, Midsummer's Eve, etc.

Even when dealing in other areas *Nationwide* consistently inflects the story back towards the idea of a national heritage. Thus, *Nationwide* will not normally deal with MPs' 'campaigns', but they will cover Willie Hamilton when he is attacking the Monarchy (30/12/75) –

> Nobody prompted a bigger response from you than Willie Hamilton . . . In January we gave him a chance . . . and asked you to reply . . .

Similarly, *Nationwide* covers, not our general economic prospects in the export trade, but the particular success of Morgan Car manufacturers – a traditional British make (17/8/76); not the economics of the EEC, but

> the effects on our great British Institutions of joining the EEC. (15/12/75.)

Here is national(-istic) politics, concern with our craft traditions and national heritage combined in a peculiarly *Nationwide* inflection: an oddly serious, yet self-parodying chauvinism. Wellings:

> Here I am in an English garden – flowers, rockery . . . and garden gnomes, good sturdy English gnomes, moulded and painted by English craftsmen . . . today their very existence is threatened by imported gnomes – 'gnomeads' . . . from Spain. How will the British gnome stand up to the new threat? (*Nationwide* 15/6/76.)

The dominant theme which orchestrates this material (in over half the items – $\frac{17}{31}$ in this category) is based on a concern with 'traditional values'. Primarily this takes the form of a massive investment in rural nostalgia – a focus on the variety of rural crafts; items on the highways and by-ways of the countryside. Implicitly there is a reference to an 'image of England' which is founded in an earlier, traditional and predominantly rural society – a more settled (even an organic) community. (See Williams 1975.)

Nationwide's peculiar addiction to the rural customs and traditions of 'Old England' finds an interesting counterpart in the cosmology of Disneyland; Dorfman and Mattelart argue that each great urban civilisation creates its own pastoral myth, an extra-social Eden, chaste and pure, where

> The only relation the centre (adult – city folk – bourgeoisie) manages to establish with the periphery (child – noble savage – worker/peasant) is touristic and sensationalist . . . The innocence of this marginal sector is what guarantees the Duckburger his touristic salvation . . . his childish rejuvenation. The primitive infrastructure offered by the Third World Countries [or, in the case of *Nationwide*, 'The Countryside'] becomes the nostalgic echo of a lost primitivism, a world of purity . . . reduced to a picture postcard to be enjoyed by a service-oriented world. (Dorfman and Mattelart 1975, p. 96.)

What *Nationwide* presents is not the rural world of agricultural production and its workaday concerns – today's price of animal feed – but the country viewed from the city, a nostalgic concern with the beauties of 'vanishing Britain ... the threat to our countryside ... ever since the Industrial Revolution' (31/3/77). Here we meet the Vicar who is concerned with the future of 'one of the Midlands' most beautiful churches' (31/3/77); the army is praised 'in an odd role – as conservationists' (5/1/76); we pay a touristic visit to Evesham and Stonehenge (18/6/76); to the West Midlands Agricultural Show (19/5/76) and the Three Counties Show (15/6/76): we observe the vestiges of the traditional cyclical calendar of rural life.

We are here presented with a very distinct set of concerns – not the workings of the local social security tribunal but of the 'Forest Verdurers Court' in the Forest of Dean (10/6/76); we learn of the work, not of factory farming, but of seaweed collectors (19/8/76); we are entreated with the problems of 'animals threatened by forest fires' (19/8/76) and see the efforts of forest fire-fighters (18/8/76). It is the world of 'Little Old England' (19/5/76) which may be treated in a 'folksy' way – often with deliberate self-parody and irony – but which is nevertheless secure, and the parody leaves the traditionalism intact.

Thus the approach to the soul-searching, investigative item 'Where have all those nice tea-places gone?' (11/6/76) – complete with music from 'An English Country Garden' – may be tongue-in-cheek, but the subject matter is ultimately accorded serious concern. After all, this is a vanishing part of our national heritage; Frank Bough: 'Does the Tradition not continue anywhere at the moment?'

But this is not all that Tradition has to offer. When the pollen count rises (10/6/76) *Nationwide* sets off the remedies of modern western medicine against the 'traditional hay fever remedies', which are explored in their regional variations around the country. Here the (regionalised) mode of treatment is as important as the subject matter: *Nationwide* uses the form again in the item on 'the ingenious artist' (5/1/76). We move into the realms of art and craft – but more particularly small, home-based craft and craft-industry. We meet individual craftspeople using 'odd materials' and working in 'unusual places' – a painter from Wales who paints family pets on stretched cobwebs, one from Leeds who paints on piano keys and one from Glasgow who paints on the inside of bottles. The *Nationwide* presentation of these activities – remnants of a craft tradition in an industrialised world – is positively celebratory. Bough sums up:

There really is no end to the extraordinarily beautiful things people do in this country. (5/1/76.)

The celebration arises directly from the contrasts which the discourse sustains; we celebrate these things because, in this mechanised world, these individuals retain the methods of painstaking individual creation, the mode of production of an earlier, valued, social formation. *Nationwide* celebrates

36

(16/8/76) the '100th anniversary of woodcarver Robert Thomson's death'; we visit the V & A craft exhibition and meet the leader of a group of women in Bristol who have painstakingly made a giant tapestry to show the town's history:

The story of Bristol, told in a very imaginative way in needle and thread. (15/6/76.)

(e) National/political news

Items on 'serious'/political issues are not generated from within *Nationwide*'s 'natural repertoire' but are externally imposed from time to time by 'hard news values'. When a dramatic news story breaks, *Nationwide* can deal with it; thus a whole studio-based *Nationwide* was devoted to the Balcombe Street siege. Similarly, on 6/1/76, although *Nationwide* had been advertising an item on compensation for road accidents the whole programme was in fact turned over to an examination of 'the Bessbrook killings' in Ireland, interviewing relatives and friends of the dead.

Thus, we may get an occasional unscheduled dedication of a whole programme to 'serious current affairs' in addition to the local news spot, but this remains atypical within the discourse of *Nationwide* during our viewing period. The programme does provide routine coverage of 'matters of national importance', but in the sample analysed these items occupy a subsidiary place – accounting for only 15% ($\frac{28}{182}$) – i.e., slightly *less* than the number of items devoted to any of the other four main categories in the discourse.

In the national/political area *Nationwide* is at its closest to the dominant forms of news and current affairs programming, and some reverence is shown towards them. This is the one area in *Nationwide* where items are predominantly dealt with in a 'straight report' format. ($\frac{15}{28}$ national/political items are dealt with in this format. This is even more marked in *Nationwide*'s local news component 'Midlands Today' where a small sample revealed the almost total dominance ($\frac{8}{11}$) of the 'straight report' format among all items.) The specificity of *Nationwide*'s presentation here often takes the form of a more 'personalised' approach by the newsreader (cf., chapter 3.vii on Mrs Barbara Carter) – stepping out of the more usual 'impartial' role to deliver personal comment on the items.

However, in the determination to 'domesticate' issues, which is the programme's preferred strategy for 'realising' national political events in terms of everyday life, *Nationwide* will 'angle' what is already structured as 'news' through the particular experience of an individual. Thus, on *Nationwide* 5/1/76 we were told that '*Panorama* will be covering the situation on British Rail later tonight'; *Nationwide*, after a brief reference to the Beeching report, went on to deal with the issue through the story of

Ron Hooper, the ex-Stationmaster of Tavistock North, who continues to live on his now disused station.

Similarly, while other current affairs programmes were analysing the successes and failures of wage controls under the social contract *Nationwide* took us to meet 'Max Quatermain, the plasterers' mate who can earn £400 p.w.' (16/8/76). When Harold Wilson resigned as Prime Minister *Nationwide*'s 'angle' on the story (16/3/76) was to show him on holiday, in his capacity as a train enthusiast.

Political activists do not regularly feature on *Nationwide*, but when there is a story like that of the 14 year old girl 'child protester' who rode into a meeting to protest about the loss of grazing rights on her local common, then it more easily finds a place in the programme. On the other hand, a case like that of Patrick Meehan (*Nationwide* 19/5/76), released from prison after seven years of a life sentence, can be dealt with on *Nationwide* in such a way that the political dimensions of the case – the accusations of framing and the involvement of British Intelligence – all but disappear. In this example *Nationwide* reconstructs the story principally as a 'drama of human suffering'. (Cf., Morley 1976, section 6.) The political background of the case disappears – all that remains is an 'exclusive interview' in close-up with a man in a highly charged emotional state two hours after being set free from the solitary block of Peterhead prison.

Again, when the story broke of the British mercenaries on trial for their lives in Angola (10/6/76), after a brief account of the relevant differences between British and Angolan Law, the story was focused primarily onto the feelings of the parents of one of the mercenaries. Similarly, in the context of the budget news (29/3/77) *Nationwide*, as noted earlier, presented the whole import of the budget through a set of interviews with 'ordinary families'. Experts enter the debate, and have the power to overrule and redefine the ordinary families' interpretations of the budget, but the whole impact of the item is predicated on the mediation of the political story through its effects on the experience of the people portrayed.

Appendix: table and notes on categorisation
Nationwide Total Sample: 29 Programmes, 182 Items

	ITEMS	World of Home and Leisure (b)		People's Problems (c)	Image of England: Town and Country (d)	National/ Political (e)	Sport	ITEM TOTAL
		(i) Leisure	(ii) Consumers					
THEMATISATION	TOTALS	40	33	30	31	28	20	182
NW Event	12	2	4	1	0	0	5	
Individual	47	20*	3	5	6	7	7	
Traditional Values	37	10	3	1	17*	4	2	
Advice	27	1	16*	6	2	0	1	
Concern and Care	16	0	0	14*	2	0	0	
Family	13	3	7	0	1	2	0	
Report	30	4	0	3	3	15*	5	
THEME TOTAL	182							

Notes on table

(1) Primary combinations of item categories and thematisation are marked * in the table.
(2) 'Nationwide Events' are, of course (see chapter 2(a)), only the tip of an iceberg composed of all inter-item links and self-referential material in the programmes. Only the 'Nationwide Events' were counted in this tabulation.
(3) There was, of course, a substantial difficulty in tabulating, for instance, the 'Family' thematisation (see notes on categorisation below) – here one is tabulating not so much an explicit presence as an implicit but recurring assumption which 'sets the frame' within which specific items are presented.

Notes on categorisation

For the purposes of this analysis the programmes in the sample were disaggregated into the individual items. Each programme item was then classified across both dimensions of the coding grid:
stage (1): by reference to the manifest content, it was assigned to an 'item' category;
stage (2): by reference to its dominant form of thematisation, it was assigned to a 'theme' category.

Both these categorisations are, of course, dependent on qualitative judgements; an item has to be judged to belong to category X (cf., Kracauer 1952). The procedure in stage (2) is somewhat more difficult, as one is assigning items to categories not by reference to the presence or absence of a particular kind of manifest content, but by reference to the presence or absence of 'propositions' (cf., Gerbner 1964) of a more general nature – theoretical constructs which are themselves unobservable. The procedure here is outlined by Gerbner as one where the task is to make explicit the implicit propositions, premises and norms which underlie and make it logically acceptable to advance a particular point of view. In this way, for instance, statements or reports may be reconstructed in terms of the propositions which underpin them; e.g., in terms of interview questions, explicating the assumptions which must be held for it to make sense to ask particular questions.
The relation of particular items to 'thematisations' or 'propositions' is necessarily problematic, and cannot be formulated on a one to one basis; thematisations can 'take as many different forms' and appear in different guises. Moreover, as Mepham argues (in Robey 1973, p. 108):

> messages are likely to be overdetermined and are thus to be analysed in terms of more than one underlying structure or proposition.

Particular items will frequently refer to more than one context, and will be an index, simultaneously, of different themes.
However, the problem of multi-accentuality that we face here is not specific

39

to this form of analysis. It is in fact the same fundamental problem which faces content analysis, proposition analysis or semiological analysis: how should we assign items to categories, statements to propositions or thematisations, and denotations to connotations?

The fundamental problem here is that of making our interpretations systematic (for all these methods rely on interpretation) and explicit; we have therefore attempted to be systematic in our categorisations. If a goes in category x, and b=a in the relevant respect, b must go in category x as well. Moreover, this has meant classifying only by reference to the dominant thematisation items which also contain other, subordinate themes. This is a form of simplification of the material; but it precisely allows us (see the dominant forms of combination, marked * in the table) to establish the basic structure of the discourse in what would otherwise remain an undifferentiated mass of multi-accentual references.

We are aware, of course, that quantification is in many respects a tool of limited use, and that one is forced towards an atomistic categorisation of data in order to provide a basis for quantification. Certainly quantification, in itself, has no scientific value; but if we are to avoid dependence on casual and fleeting impressions, or generalisation from analyses of single instances, then quantification is of some use. While in no sense constituting a final test or 'proof' it does facilitate a measure of check on our interpretations; through quantification we have aimed to establish the basic profile and contours of the distribution of the different elements of the *Nationwide* discourse in our sample. In some respects this procedure has meant simply replicating immediate impressions through laborious means – for instance, the fact that 'stories of individuals' were important to *Nationwide* was immediately obvious on an impressionistic level. However, it is one thing to assert that as an impression, and another to demonstrate that that kind of thematisation in fact accounts for nearly 30% ($\frac{47}{182}$) of the stories in our sample, and that this thematisation is precisely dominant in the 'world of leisure' ($\frac{20}{40}$ items).

Our analysis, in this section, then, has disaggregated items from their individual programme-contexts and treated them as elements in the larger discourse of *Nationwide*, over and above the level of the programme. We would argue that this has precisely allowed us to trace some of the contours of that larger discourse – by mapping the dominant and recurrent distribution of the elements and their recurrent forms of combination, over a long period. In the next chapter we move on to complement this analysis of the overall discourse with a partial analysis of the internal structure of one edition.

3 Linking and Framing: *Nationwide* in Action 19/5/76

(i) Introduction

So far we have been drawing our illustrations from a wide selection of *Nationwide* materials, based on notes made during an extended period of viewing. In this section, we take a closer look at *'Nationwide* in Action', concentrating exclusively on the edition of 19th May 1976. The chapter is in two parts. First, we offer a more detailed breakdown and outline of some parts of the *Nationwide* 'script'; secondly, we offer a commentary on certain aspects of the *Nationwide* discourse. We try here to make available the information on which our categorisation of the items in this and other programmes is based, and to explain the way in which we approached the programme. We fully recognise that our analysis fails to examine in detail the 'programme as a whole' at both the visual and verbal levels. A fully adequate analysis would need to provide an account of the structure of the programme at both these levels, and, preferably, a full programme transcript with visual references. This is beyond the scope of our present endeavour – we offer here a schematic outline of the programme which is no more than the beginning of a full analysis.

We begin with a brief description of the 19th May 1976 programme with some of our own comments on items. We then try to deconstruct the common sense notion of *Nationwide* being 'about' its items by printing a descriptive transcript of the programme, 'foregrounding' all the studio links and item introductions, providing full transcript of these, but giving only brief specifications for the items themselves. There are several reasons for this procedure. First, links, introductions and frame make, in our view, a major contribution to holding the programme together, imposing on its varied 'menu' a distinctive identity and unity. Second, the introductions were important for the whole of our analysis because they frequently signal what the main topic or angle of the item is 'for *Nationwide*'. Thus, in introducing an item, *Nationwide* frequently establishes its own 'take' on a topic – it does not simply transmit items, it constructs itself as a very specific kind of discourse by its production of *Nationwide* items, or by the active work of appropriating a topic or item into the characteristic *Nationwide* discourse. Our own assignment of items to categories was made mainly on the basis of how they were characterised in the 'links discourse'. For example, it seemed to us important that 'local news' – with its regional flavour and inflection – is invariably designated as such; Ralph Nader is introduced as 'America's leading campaigner on consumer affairs' (consumers); Mrs Carter (see below) is introduced as an individual with a special interest (leisure); etc.

Introductions and links also play a key role in the thematising of items. Thematisation is, of course, different from identifying the topic of an item, as the same topic can be 'thematised' in a number of different ways. Thematisation is inevitably a more difficult part of the analysis than the assignment of items to topics, and is less open to examination without reference to a transcript of the whole programme. We saw both the items referred to above as thematised through 'individuals'; in the case of Mrs

Carter, through the stress on her individual feelings and experience, in the case of Nader, through the emphasis on his individual role in 'consumer campaigns'.

In general, we adopted this approach, and have chosen to highlight the discourse strategies most directly connected with these aspects of the programme, because of the importance we have come to attach to the 'links discourse' (see chapter 2.iii(a)). On an initial viewing, the links may seem to carry no meaning in themselves other than their explicit function of 'linking items'. The links proclaim their own transparency: they are reduced to their apparent function of dependency on the items they precede and succeed. But we would argue, in fact, that the links are what centrally structure and constitute the programme discourse. It is in the links that the main strategies of the discourse can be most clearly observed.

The linking/introductory statements are usually made in direct address to the audience, and indeed these are the only sections of the programme discourse which speak (in a kind of meta-dialogue) directly to the audience – explaining what will appear on the programme, who 'we' will meet, etc. – and it is the *Nationwide* team who have exclusive access to this level of discourse. In anticipating and commenting on items, the links assign items to specific contexts of meaning and association. Thus Mrs Carter, through her 'localness', is primarily placed within the programme's continuing search for 'everyday drama':

> I wonder if you remember this dramatic picture we showed you a few weeks ago of Mrs Barbara Carter of Halesowen . . .

It is 'our' memory, as regular members of the *Nationwide* audience, which carries meaning. The links thus constantly produce the meaning of 'Nation-wideness', which is, in its turn, grounded in a specific image of the audience-as-nation, sharing with the presenters a common-sense understanding of the social world.

(ii) Programme description and script 19/5/76

(i) Summary

Time (Mins.)	Item	Comments
00	Regional Menu	} Use of identification pronouns: 'we meet'/'the person who' . . .
02	National Menu	
	NEWS 'MIDLANDS TODAY'	
03	Shop steward at Coventry car plant sacked. Walsall firm cleared of charges of failing to protect their workers. Plessey management give ultimatum to workers in pay dispute.	A 'package' of industrial news. All brief reports except for that on the carpet firm, which includes film, and some 'background'/ information.
(06)	Kidderminster carpet firm in danger of closure. Earth tremor in Stoke-on-Trent.	
	Mrs B. Carter goes back to meet the lions who attacked her in a West Midlands Safari Park.	Questioned exclusively about her feelings. C.U. on facial expressions.
	NEWS Cheltenham policeman praised by coroner for bravery. West Midlands Agricultural Show, Shrewsbury. 6 workers at Rolls Royce Coventry win £200,000 on pools.	Photo stereotype of 'striking workers' redefined by commentators as 'individual success'.
13	Interview with Ralph Nader on consumer affairs.	'Devil's advocate' interview probing Nader's credibility.
15	WEATHER REPORT	Use of child's drawing.
	Report on a new invention from a Midlands College which will enable blind students to produce 3-D drawings.	} Both items focus on the role of 'technological development'; visual emphasis on machinery in C.U. Implicit contrast made between obvious value of the invention in former item and the dubious value of the latter project.
	Report on a group of design students from Wolverhampton who've been building a 'Survival Kit' out of rubbish material.	
	NATIONAL *NATIONWIDE*	
25	*NW* team members go on boat trip on the yacht 'Nationwide' on the Norfolk Broads.	Self-reflexive item: the *NW* team become the 'actors' in their own story.
28	A report on American servicemen and their families on a U.S. base in Suffolk.	Extensive use of stereotypes of 'Englishness'/'Americanness' in report on 'invasion' of 'Little Old England'.

45

Time (Mins.)	Item	Comments
37	Interview with Patrick Meehan, released from jail with a free pardon after being originally convicted of murder.	Focusing on the subject's feelings: CU on facial expressions.
40 50	What to wear/eat/drink at the races. The *Nationwide* Horse: Realin. Report on the financial problems of English racing. Interview with Clement Freud, a racehorse owner.	The 'Sport of Kings' brought to the *NW* audience; a highly composite item involving studio mock up, outdoor film, graphics & studio interview.

(ii) Transcript

REGIONAL MENU

Tom Coyne: (See fig. 4.) Good evening. Tonight we meet the students who built a new life for themselves out of a load of rubbish – these might look like a few old plastic bags to you but actually for a time it was home to them. And then we join the lady who was attacked by the lions in the Safari Park as she goes back again to meet the lions. That's us at six.

NATIONAL MENU

Michael Barratt: (See fig. 5.) And after your own programmes we go cruising down the river to bring you our third programme from East Anglia. We also meet the Americans whose home is in Suffolk this bicentennial year and we consider the crisis in racing. Our own horse is looking good, but the sport of kings itself is in trouble and we ask Clement Freud what's to be done about it Nationwide.

'MIDLANDS TODAY' INTRODUCTION

TC: Well you know, isn't it marvellous, every time you come outside the studio the rain seems to come with you. I think that what we've done with this kind of programme is to create a new kind of rain dance ha ha but I'll tell you one thing it certainly isn't going to bother David Stevens because he's back inside waiting to read the news.

Item	Technical Specification	Speaker Status	Categorisation	Thematisation
Shop steward sacked	Studio Report d/a	Newsreader	Local News: Industrial/ Political (e)	'Straight' Report
Walsall firm cleared	Film Report v/o	Newsreader	Local News: Ind./Pol. (e)	'Straight' Report
Plessey ultimatum to workers	Studio Report d/a	Newsreader	Local News: Ind./Pol. (e)	'Straight' Report
Report on carpet firm	Film Report v/o	Reporter	Local News: Ind./Pol. (e)	'Straight' Report
Earth tremor	Studio Report d/a	Newsreader	Local News: Ind./Pol. (e) : other	'Straight' Report

Item	Technical Specification	Speaker Status	Categorisation	Thematisation

TC: Well there's going to be more news of course later in the programme. I wonder if you remember this dramatic picture we showed you a few weeks ago of Mrs Barbara Carter of Halesowen. She was attacked by lions in the West Midlands Safari park. Well after an experience like that you'd hardly expect Mrs Carter to be keen on uh seeing lions again. But today she visited a farm near Stratford on Avon to do just that. A report from Alan Towers:

Item	Technical Specification	Speaker Status	Categorisation	Thematisation
Lady & Lion (See fig.6.)	Field Interview	Intvwr. & Participant	Leisure (b)	Individual

David Stevens: A much braver and a more determined person that I could ever be.

Item	Technical Specification	Speaker Status	Categorisation	Thematisation
Police Constable	Studio Report d/a	Newsreader	Local News (e)	'Straight' Report

DS: Two stories of bravery.

Item	Technical Specification	Speaker Status	Categorisation	Thematisation
Agricultural show	Film Report v/o	Newsreader	Rural England (d)	'Straight' Report
Pools winners (See fig. 7.)	Studio Report & still d/a	Newsreader	Leisure (e)	'Straight' Report

TC: I'll tell you something, it's cold out here tonight, just in case you always thought I looked blue like this.
You know America's leading campaigner on consumer affairs, Ralph Nader, uh was in the Midlands today, was here to speak at an Industrial Safety Exhibition which was held at the National Exhibition Centre, and it's reported that Mr Nader was paid a fee of £2,000 for speaking. There to meet him was Geoffrey Greene:

Item	Technical Specification	Speaker Status	Categorisation	Thematisation
Nader Interview (See fig.8.)	Field Interview	Intwvr. & Expert (Soc.)	Consumer (b.ii)	Individual

TC: Well with the drizzle coming down, I hardly dare mention it, but let's take a look at our weatherpicture. It comes from Leicester, and from Jane Hickman, who's 15 years of age:

Item	Technical Specification	Speaker Status	Categorisation	Thematisation
Weather	Studio d/a	Intwvr. & Expert (Soc.)		Individual

(See fig. 9.) The weather: well, the showers or periods of rain, heavy at times, will gradually die out from the West to give clear intervals later in the night. Minimum temperature 6 degrees Centigrade. Tomorrow we'll have some sunny intervals with further showers developing. There will be winds, the sort you can hear in the microphone now, westerly, light or moderate. And that's it.

Now one of the things you'd hardly expect a blind person to be able to do is draw a picture like the one we've just seen. But things of course are changing all the time, the new development that is being tried out here in Birmingham could certainly change all that. Here's a report now from Duncan Gibbens:

DG: The man who's patented the drawing board is Mr Christopher Vincent. As head of the Technical Graphics division of Birmingham Polytechnic, he's adapted the board from a perspective grid. Now he hopes to introduce his device into other colleges for the blind.

Item		Technical Specification	Speaker Status	Categorisation	Thematisation
Blind students learn to draw (See figs. 10–13.)	Report on invention	Film Report v/o	Reporter	People's problems (c)	Concern and care
	Interview with inventor	Field Interview	Interviewer and expert		
	Interview with student	Field Interview	Interviewer and participants		
	Report on students' prospects	Film Report v/o	Reporter		

DG: Soon 3-Dimensional braille maps will be developed using drawings from the board. Then blind youngsters like Paul and Martin Sullivan will not only have a better understanding of the way the world looks – they'll be able to find their way around much more easily.

TC: (See fig. 14.) If our society was destroyed, heaven forbid, I wonder if you could pick up the threads of life and build a new one for yourself out of the rubbish lying around? Well, a group of students from the Wolverhampton Polytechnic have just survived that sort of experience in Wales. They're design students and one of the tutors behind it is Mr Wyn Foot. (What's it all about?)

Interview with course tutor on project	Field Interview	Intwr. & Expert	People's problems (c)	Individuals

TC: Good. Well, what I'll do, I'll move across actually to have a word with some of the students over here. As we've just heard from Mr Foot all the objects lying around came from rubbish dumps and places, discarded by industry and householders and all that sort of thing.

Interview with female student	Field Interview	Intwr. & Participant	People's problems (c)	Individuals

TC: Well look, I'll leave you carrying on working there. . . Are you all right in there. . . Good, you look well. Let's move across here now and talk to this erum gentleman.

Interview male student (See fig. 15.)	Field Interview	Intwr. & Participant	People's problems (c)	Individuals

TC: Well thank you very much indeed and thank you all for coming and reconstructing the scene, for it's been a pleasure talking to you, and now let's go to Norwich.

Item	Technical Specification	Speaker Status	Categorisation	Thematisation

NATIONWIDE INTRODUCTION

Michael Barratt: For the third time this week welcome to the Norwich studio of the BBC, the 'LOOK EAST' studio, because for the third time *Nationwide* is coming to you from East Anglia as indeed it's gonna be all week. Well, we've had a jolly good week so far here and I've enjoyed it immensely; it's my last night of course at the table here. We haven't really had any alarms or er real worries. (*Ian Masters:* no, no) up to now (very true). Actually let me let the viewers into a secret because this morning Ian and I and Bob Wellings went out onto the Broads, onto the River Ure, is it, that comes into Norwich?

IM: The Yer.

MB: The Yure?

IM: The Yerr.

MB: I see, I see, the River Ure, and we went out on that and we were going to pretend that *Nationwide* was starting on a boat. Well *Nationwide* in a way is going to start on a boat in a few minutes because we had some problems with the film. Anyway Ian and Bob and I would like to welcome you a second time to *Nationwide*.

MB: (See fig. 16.) And er welcome again to East Anglia for the third night this week and in a rather different style this time. *Nationwide* as you can see is seaborne and this is a very ener. . . Stand by? What do you mean?

IM: Stand by to go about, Mike.

MB: Oh I see.

IM: Let that rope go back and hold onto the other one. Come forrard.

MB: Let it go? Right.

(Noise)

IM: That's fine.

MB: I say, where's Bob? Bob, where are you?

BW: Messing about in a boat. Such fun.

IM: The trouble is that when you're sailing in trees . . . it suddenly comes from behind the tree and hits you hard. It's a lot easier to sail to Holland; as a matter of fact the chap, this a pal of mine, does it all the time.

MB: Does he? A bit boring, isn't it?

IM: Yes . . . Well, he enjoys it. . . (Laughter)

MB: (Obscured) Right, do I let go now?

Item	Technical Specification	Speaker Status	Categorisation	Thematisation

IM: Er, listen, we're catching some wind. Bob, where are you? Bob, come on, give us a hand, mate. What are you doing down. . .? Come on, Bob, will you put that main sheet on the cleet?

BW: The cleet?

IM: On the cleet. The mainsheet, yes. Well come on, Bob; no, that's the railing, Bob.

BW: That? This?

IM: That's the railing. No, that's the gibsheet.

BW: Ian . . .

IM: Were you listening to what I was saying?

BW: Wh-wh-wh-what do you want me to do?

IM: I want you to get . . .

MB: Hey, we're going about or tacking or something.

IM: No, no. Keep on holding it in.

MB: Right. My fingers are still sore, you know.

BW: All this 'tacking' and 'avast' and 'ahoy' and left hand down and giblets and spinnakers and god know what . . . ugh, here we go again – ludicrous performance.

MB: And while we move on with Bob up river to Norwich and the studio let's hear from another part of East Anglia, from Suffolk this time although you might think it was bit of America. In Bicentennial year a report from Luke Casey in Leighton Heath:

LC: This is part of a very polite invasion. Three times a week an American aircraft courteously deposits its cargo of United States citizens onto this seasoned soil of Britain. For most, East Anglia is their first, jet-lagged look at Little Old England, where even the language is different. Soon they'll be happily, if predictably, pitching into the battle between tomatoes and tomātoes, and the mystery of Worcestershire Sauce. But first, they learn of our more pressing eccentricities.

Report on Americans' arrival	Film Report v/o	Reporter	England (d)	Traditional Values

LC: Not all the newcomers though, feel they can't live without their instant America kits. This old English farmhouse is home for one family.

Interview with Mrs Pat Pfleiger (See fig. 17.)	Field Interview	Interviewer & Participant	England (d)	Traditional Values

LG: Pat Pfleiger; her husband Dave's a major at Mildenhall, and their three children are not the sort of people who'd like to see Coca-Cola on the moon. The breakfast of hot-dogs and French toast is the only recognisable concession to their American-ness. (See fig. 18.)

Item	Technical Specification	Speaker Status	Categorisation	Thematisation
Interview with Dave Pfleiger	Field Interview	Interviewer & Participant	England (d)	Traditional Values
Report on Americans in E. Anglia	Film report v/o	Reporter		

LC: It may not be cricket, but it's sure as hell American.

MB: Luke Casey there, among the nice people in America, or was it Suffolk. This afternoon, as you may have heard, Patrick Meehan was released from prison in Peterhead, so over now to David Scott in Aberdeen:

DS: Meehan was released from prison after seven years. Most of it had been spent in solitary confinement as a protest against his conviction. It was just under two hours ago that he was released from Peterhead prison, and he was quickly reunited with his former wife Betty, and their son Gary. We recorded this exclusive interview a short time ago.

Item	Technical Specification	Speaker Status	Categorisation	Thematisation
Interview with Meehan (See figs 19–20.)	Field Interview	Interviewer & Participant	National/ Political (e)	Individual

MB: Patrick Meehan filmed exclusively for *Nationwide* by our colleagues in BBC Scotland. Patrick Meehan who of course has served seven years of a life sentence for murder – a conviction based yet again on identification evidence. And now back to our base for this week. East Anglia of course is the home of *Nationwide's* adopted racehorse Realin, so we thought that tonight we'd go racing.

Item	Technical Specification	Speaker Status	Categorisation	Thematisation
Bob Wellings at the races (See fig 21.)	Studio d/a	Reporter	Sport	Traditional Values
Nationwide Horse (See fig. 22.)	Outdoor d/a	Reporter		
Problems of English Racing	Film & Graphics v/o	Nat. Presenter		

MB: Well now, Clement Freud in London, that's all a great pity but, er, most people do expect to pay for their sport, why should racehorse owners be different?

Item	Technical Specification	Speaker Status	Categorisation	Thematisation
Interview with Clement Freud (See fig. 23.)	Studio Interview	National Presenter & Institutional Represen- tative	Sport	Traditional Values

MB: Something which clearly makes you, Clement Freud, very sad, but thank you very much for explaining it for me. Well, that's all; as I was saying this is my, er, last night with you, Ian Masters from Norwich here and from East Anglia. I've enjoyed it very much. Frank Bough will be back in this chair tomorrow night, of course (cough) I've got an awful frog in my throat now, anyway from me until tomorrow: Goodnight. (See fig. 24.)

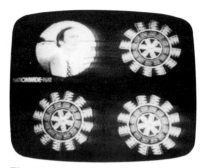

Fig. 1: *Nationwide* logo

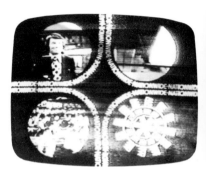

Fig. 2: *Nationwide* logo

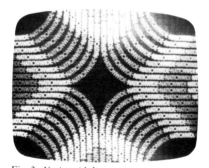

Fig. 3: *Nationwide* logo

Fig. 4: Tom Coyne introducing menu for 'Midlands Today'

Fig. 5: Michael Barratt introducing menu for *Nationwide*

Fig. 6: Interview with Mrs Carter and lion

Fig. 7: Pools winners

Fig. 8: Ralph Nader

Fig. 9: Weather report

Fig. 10: Blind students in the classroom

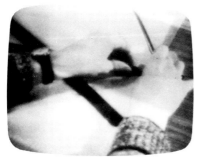

Fig. 11: Blind students—the invention at work

Fig. 12: Blind students interviewed

Fig. 13: Blind students—close of item

Fig. 14: Students' rubbish project—introduction

Fig. 15: Students' rubbish project—interview

Fig. 16: Michael Barratt and regional presenter on the *Nationwide* boat

Fig. 17: Interview with Mrs Pfleiger

Fig. 18: The Pfleigers at breakfast

Fig. 19: Interview with Patrick Meehan (*i*)

Fig. 20: Interview with Patrick Meehan (*ii*)

Fig. 21: Bob Wellings at the races

Fig. 22: Val Singleton introduces the *Nationwide* horse

Fig. 23: Michael Barratt interviewing Clement Freud

Fig. 24: Michael Barratt closes the programme

Content Categories	Thematisations
(a) Nationwide Events/links	Self-Referential/Identification
(b.i) Leisure	Individuals
(b.ii) Consumers	Advice/family
(c) People's problems	Concern and care
(d) Image of England	Traditional values
(e) National/Political; Sport	Straight report

Technical Specifications

Direct address (d/a) { Studio Report / Outdoor

Film Report { Voice over (vo) / Reporter to Camera

Interview { Studio / Field

Studio Discussion

Speaker Status Categories

Presenter — National / Regional

Newsreader
Reporter
Interviewer

} Programme Internal

Participant
Eyewitness
Institutional
Representation
Politician
Expert

} Programme External

(iii) The links

Everything is 'linked in'; an item cannot appear on *Nationwide* without having been firmly set in context. First, it will be introduced by being located in the structure of the programme text (cf., Halliday 1973, p. 66); it is made clear what part of the programme we are in (Regional/National *Nationwide*), how the item relates to other parts of the programme. Second, it is made clear how it relates to our concerns in the social world.

This can usefully be seen as a four or five stage strategy:

(1) *Linking* — performing the textual function, guiding us through the programme discourse ('now, over to . . .').

(2) *Framing* — establishing the topic and its relevance to the concerns of the audience.

(3) *Focusing* — establishing the particular angle that the programme is going to take on the topic.

If there are to be extra-programme participants a fourth stage is necessary:

(4) *Nominating* — clueing the audience in as to the identity of extra-programme participants or interviewees; establishing their 'status' (expert, eyewitness, etc.) and their right/competence to speak on the topic in question – thus establishing their (proposed) degree of 'credibility'/authority within the discourse.

— *Nationwide* members, of course, also have their 'statuses' continually marked and established within the discourse ('our reporter in Lakenheath. . .') but they are also pre-given as established figures, with an established competence (e.g., Barratt) and role in the programme.

Customarily there is a fifth stage of the process:

(5) *Summing-up* — drawing together the main threads of the item, its relevance and the context in which it is to be placed; done by the interviewer at the end of the item (internally), and/or by the linkman, before going on to introduce the next item.

If we look at the item on the blind students who have been able to learn to draw because of a new invention we can see this process in operation:

| (1) *Link :* | 'One of the things you wouldn't expect a blind person to be able to do is draw . . . a picture like the one we've just seen but things of course are | The link is given by the regional presenter; he links its relevance back to the previous item (a child's drawing of the weather) and frames/connects it with |
| (2) *Frame* | changing all the time, and a new invention . . . could change all that.' | our social concern for the blind. |

He then introduces/nominates the reporter who is going to do the story:

He then introduces/nominates the reporter who is going to do the story:

'. . . a report now from Duncan Gibbons.'

who moves on to phase (3) of the process:

(3) *Focusing:*

'A class at . . . College for the Blind . . . these youngsters are working with a new device . . . giving them a remarkable insight into the world of the sighted person. The device is a new drawing board . . .'

He focuses our concern with the topic onto the specific role of a new invention in helping blind people to produce 3-D drawings.

He goes on to explain a little how the device works and then moves to phase (4):

(4) *Nominating:*

'The man who invented the drawing board is Mr Christopher Vincent, head of technical graphics at Birmingham Polytechnic . . . he adapted it from a perspective grid . . . hopes to introduce the device into other colleges for the blind. . .

He thus nominates the first extra-programme participant – he introduces him and explains his status as expert/inventor, and thus his competence to speak on the topic.

The inventor is then interviewed, and afterwards two of the students who are using the invention. At the end of the interview with the students we move out to a film report of them walking cumbersomely out of the college, arm in arm, and the reporter, in voice-over, sums up:

(5) *Summing-up:*

'Soon 3-D maps will be developed using drawings from the board. Then blind youngsters like . . . [these] will be able to find their way around much more easily.'

The summing up contextualises the item in terms of its social use-value; the invention will help to produce maps which will practically improve the lives of the blind students.

This item, then, displays a recurring *Nationwide* structure:

(L	F	(N)	Fo	N	(. . . .)	F)
(Link	Frame	(Nominate)	Focus	Nominate	(. . . .)	Frame)

The structure contains (in both senses: includes, and holds within its limits) the independent-authentic contributions of the extra-programme partici-pants. That is, it defines and determines the structure of how, where and what the extra-programme participants can contribute. Of course, the items appear to ground, witness and authenticate themselves, outside the pro-gramme, in the 'real world' through these 'extra-programme' contributions. This process of authentication is supported and realised by the forms in which the participants' accounts are signified: that is, participants are shown 'in their own person' on film; what they are said to be doing is witnessed to by our seeing, in the visuals, that they are indeed doing it; and they are shown and heard, speaking 'in their own voice'. But this apparent transcripted reality is itself framed by the encoding structure of the item, which establishes its own over-determining 'reality'; and, through the visual and verbal commentary, encodes, as its privileged reading, a specific interpretation of what they are saying and doing. The discursive work of linking and framing items binds the divergent realities of these different items into the 'reality' of the programme itself – reconstitutes them in terms of their reality-for-the-programme. Over against the divergent times, histories and locations of these different items, the linking work establishes its own privileged continuity – incorporates them into the 'natural' *Nationwide* flow, into *Nationwide* time. Essentially, *Nationwide* as a programme is articulated through these two axes: the axis of *difference* (different items, different topics, different participants – each with its own register, its own point of interest, contributing to the panoramic *variety* which is *Nationwide*'s manifest stock-in-trade, its claim to be a magazine topicality programme); the axis of *continuity and combination* – which binds, links and frames these differences into a continuous, connected, flowing 'unity'. But the linking discourse has a determining primacy in the hierarchy over the other discourses, which are actively subordinated to it through certain specific discursive strategies.

It would be perhaps more appropriate to define the linking and framing discourse as the *meta-language* of the programme – that which comments on and places the other discourses in a hierarchy of significance, and which therefore actively constitutes the programme as a 'structure in dominance'.

As we move through any one item – from direct address, through filmed report and interview, to studio discussion – we move from that level of the discourse at which control is most directly in the presenter's hands, to that at which the structure is more 'open'. This movement, however, is paralleled by an increasing restriction of access as we move up the scale: only the *Nationwide* team have access to the level of the discourse in which frames and contextualisations for all the elements of an item are given. Extra-programme participants only have access to the lower levels of the discourse; and their contributions are always framed by the presenter's statements.

(iv) Verbal and visual discourses: combinations and closures

The framing of items is also set by the relations of hierarchy established between the visual and verbal levels of discourse. The use of voice-over film reports – where the commentary 'explains' the meaning and significance of the images shown – is the most tightly-controlled form in which the 'actuality' material is presented: here, the verbal discourse is positively privileged over the visual. It is important, analytically, to hold a distinction between these two, distinct, signifying chains. The visuals could, potentially, be 'read' by some section of the audience outside of or against the interpretive work which the commentary (voice-over) or meta-language suggests. But the dominant tendency – which the specific work of combination accomplishes here – is for the visual images to be 'resolved' into those dominant meanings and interpretations which the commentary is providing. This interpretive work is, however, repressed or occluded by the synchronisation of voice-over with images, which makes it appear as if the images 'speak for themselves' – declare their own transparent meaning, without exterior intervention. This synchronisation of discources is the work of *coupling* – the accomplishment of a particular combination of discourses which has the effect of *fixing* certain privileged meanings to the images, binding the two signifying chains together in a specific relation of 'dominance'. Specifically, film used on *Nationwide*, although it may have its own faint sound-track (naturalistic background sound, for example), is invariably *voiced-over* for some part of an item, except where the *Nationwide* team itself (e.g., the East Anglia boat trip) is the 'subject' of the item, providing both the content of, as well as the commentary on, the report. In that situation, sound is relayed direct.

Thus, there is a repeating structure which (to take examples from the 19 May programme) is used for both the 'Blind' and the 'American' items:

(introduction – v/o film report)

(interview(s))

(conclusion – v/o film report)

As in the case of framing by direct address, v/o introductions set the frame and dominant meaning within which the content of an item or interview is set.

This structure can be seen at work if we look at the item on 'Blind students' – now with special attention to the visual discourse. Visually, this item has a complex form: we begin with v/o film report, showing the invention in use in a classroom – we see and hear students performing operations which we do not yet understand. The indeterminacy or unresolved nature of this visual 'clue' is sustained in the v/o commentary:

Reporter: 'This/mysterious/clicking noise makes this a very special classroom.'

This temporary 'suspense-effect' is quickly resolved, as the commentary begins to explain the meaning of these unintelligible visual messages. We then see film without commentary (in direct sound) of an obviously authoritative figure (this much is signified by his manner, dress; age, style of addressing and directing the students), moving around the classroom. After a few seconds – in which the visual resolution is, once again, temporarily suspended – the reporter's commentary identifies him:

Reporter: 'The man who's patented the drawing board is Mr . . . .'

We then move on to more film of the invention in use, with v/o commentary – this time, an internal commentary, providing by the inventor himself – and then to a shot of the inventor being interviewed, speaking now direct to camera.

In these sections of the item, visual sequencing reinforces (and also constitutes) the force of the meaning of the images: while the inventor is talking, explaining how the invention works and how he derived the idea for it, the camera gives us detailed close-ups of the use and workings of the invention: shots of hands moving along T-squares, etc.

When we move, however, to speak to the students themselves, the camera zooms in to a facial close-up, as soon as they begin to speak of the difference the invention has made to their personal lives. Here the emphasis is fixed, visually, on one student (on his facial expression) as he explains how the invention has changed his life. The use of visual close-up on the face – expressing in personal terms the essential-human 'point' of the item – supports the displacement of focus from the technical to the experiential register.

For the final section of the item (third move in the structure), as we watch the blind students leaving the college, the students walk away from us out of the door, the camera moving back to allow us a more distanced/'objective' perspective – a concluding, rounding-out, closing shot. The reporter sums up and contextualises the significance of the item *as a whole*, in v/o commentary, over the 'closing' filmed images.

(v) Setting the spectator in place: positions of knowledge

It is clear from this brief analysis that no permanent dominance is given to the visual in the hierarchy of discourses established in this item. Rather, we would have to say that, at the key points of transition in the item, a dominant interpretation is, if anything, 'privileged' by the signifying discourse of the commentary and v/o meta-language. However, certain key transitions *are* principally realised through the shift from one visual register to another – for example, the *technical* aspect of the item is 'shown' by the close-ups of hands manipulating the apparatus, before its 'workings' are explained by an internal commentary; the transition from the technical to the *experiential* register is principally accomplished by the camera movement to full-face visual close-up; the 'closure' of the item, and its 'human significance', is pointed principally by the camera pulling back to give us a more 'overall' view of what has been accomplished for the blind students coupled, of course, with a framing commentary. What matters, then, is not the permanent primacy of the visual discourse, but rather the way the verbal-visual hierarchy of combinations is differently established at different moments or points in the item – the discursive work which each on its own and both together accomplishes and sustains.

The visual discourse, however, has a special significance in *positioning* the spectator, setting him/her in place in a set of shifting positions-of-knowledge with respect to the item. Even here, positioning ought not to be reduced to the specific technical movements of camera shot and angle, but must rather be understood as the result of the combined visual-verbal 'work' – sustained by and realised through the programme's discursive operations.

Thus, when we first 'look' at the invention being used in the classroom, we look at this scene with and through the 'eye' of the presenter. It is his 'gaze' which we follow, from a position – a perspective on the filmed scene – outside the frame, looking in on it. Here, paradoxically, we 'see' from an absent but marked position, which is where the presenter's *voice* appears to come from: 'this mysterious clicking noise . . .'

It is the 'gaze' of the presenter/spectator, outside the programme, which 'finds' the inventor, within the frame; which then picks up and follows (as the camera does) his 'glance'. The spectator's position is now, through a mirror-reciprocation, identified with that of the inventor's as we look at what he looks at – and he can now directly address 'us'; an identical line of vision, from inside the frame to 'us' outside the frame, has been established. This privileged giving-of-the-commentary over to a representative figure within the frame (operating along this line of vision) is sustained by the specific work of designation, presenter-to-inventor. That is, it is sustained by the *process* through which, progressively, the various positions of the viewer are established: the overseeing 'look' at the film, from a position outside its system of significations; the 'finding' of a position of identification for the spectator (outside), inside the film-space; the mirror-effect, which, having established 'us' at the centre of the film – seeing what is to be seen, through its glance – then enables the reciprocating look, back at us, through direct address, eye-to-eye. Our 'look' is now identical with 'his' (the inventor's). Hence, while, as he speaks, he looks down and around at the operations which he is explicating, 'we' follow his glance; we have been inscribed in it, and take the perspective of his look: close-ups of the invention, hands moving along T-squares, feeling their way . . .

The transition to the students speaking and imaged 'as themselves' returns us to a position outside the frame – but a privileged one; a point emphasised by the camera zoom, manipulating the distances, which 'takes us closer in' – but which is also a shift of focus in the other sense, obliterating the technical details of the classroom, and 'focusing' (or re-focusing) our 'look' on what is now the most important element – the expressive signifier of the face of the subject, in what has been abstracted/emphasised (by the zoom) as the essence, the truth, the human point, of the item: technology changes lives; it enables the blind to 'see'; we 'see' that it does, because we see the intense (i.e., intensified, by the close angle) meaning-for-the-subject of what has already been shown.

The point once made, in its most intensified moment/point of registration, we are ready for the closure. Closure is signified here by re-positioning the spectator in the place of a now more-inclusive knowledge – in the enclosing, framing, gathering-together plenitude of our 'sense of a sufficient and necessary ending'. 'They' – the subjects of the item – are seen moving away from us, from our position of knowledge/vision; we, in turn, move back from this involvement (i.e., are moved back, as the camera retreats, from the point of intensity), to get a retrospective-circumscribing 'over-look' of the item: what it *all* means . . .

What we 'know' about the 'Blind' item is inscribed through the process of *how* we come to know – that is, the positions from which we see and hear what there is to be known about this item. That knowledge is constructed in part through the inscription of the spectator-as-subject in a series of positions – positions of vision, positions of knowledge – sustained by and realised in the discursive operations. These operations set us in place in a process of knowledge – from perplexed ignorance ('this mysterious clicking noise . . .') to completed, circumscribed understanding (what the item was *really* all about). The ideological effect of this item is not in any sense completed by this process of positioning – it includes, for example, what we 'come to know' about humane technology, about how lives are changed; but it depends, in part, on how the process of 'coming to know' is sustained through the programme's discursive work – constituting the spectator actively in the unity of the places in which 'we' are successively fixed and positioned.

(vi) Speaker status and the structure of access: subject and experts

Access to the discourse is controlled by the programme team. The question is 'access on what terms for whom' and the crucial variable here is the extra-programme status of participants. Participants of 'low' status will tend (a) to be questioned only about their 'feelings' and responses to issues whose terms have already been defined (cf., Cardiff 1974) and (b) will tend also to be quickly cut short if they move 'off the point'. Those of 'higher' status will conversely tend to be (a) questioned about their 'ideas' rather than their 'feelings' and (b) will be allowed much more leeway to define issues in their own terms.

This distinction is formally supported by the tendency to move in for bigger close-ups of subjects who are revealing their feelings, whereas the set-up for the 'expert' is usually the same as that for the interviewer – the breast pocket shot. Both kinds of statused participants are 'nominated' by the reporters into the discourse, questioned by a member of the team, and have their contributions framed and 'summed-up'.

Thus, there is a clear differentiation in the discourse between those participants who appear, principally, as 'subjects' – something newsworthy has happened to them – and those who appear as 'expert' in some particular field. The distinction between the two types of participants is constructed through the interview questions.

Thus, in the case of those who appear as newsworthy subjects it is their feelings and experiences which are explored:

(1) to lady attacked by lion: 'How did you feel . . . when this attack took place? You must have literally thought it was your end, did you?'

(2) to blind students learning to draw: '. . . what sort of difference has this drawing system made to your everyday life?'

When we meet 'experts' of various kinds it is their ideas and explanations that are of interest, not their feelings as 'human subjects':

(1) to inventor of drawing system: 'Did it come as a surprise to you to learn that blind people had a perspective?'

(2) to Nader: 'What are your ideas, for instance, on industrial safety?'

Interviewees whose status is constructed as being low (either – in the case of Patrick Meehan, – because of his background or – in the case of the lecturer who organised the 'rubbish/survival kit' project – because of a lack of clear legitimacy in their particular (in this case educational) field of practice) can be easily cut short if they go 'off the point'.

In the case of the lecturer, Tom Coyne as interviewer feels able to demand that he give an account of himself in a way that forces him to comply. Thus after a brief introduction to the item Coyne asks crisply:

What's it all about?

to which the lecturer feels bound to respond, half-apologetically:

Lecturer: 'Um, I think I should explain . . .'

However, he fails to provide an explanation which meets Coyne's fundamental questioning of the validity of the project, and is cut short in favour of interviews with the students who 'actually went to the rubbish dump'.

When an interviewee is considered to have some more considerable status – as in the case of Ralph Nader in this programme – he will be allowed more time to develop his answers to questions; he cannot be cut short so brusquely and may even be allowed the 'space' to redefine the questions asked into his own terms. Greene questions Nader quite sharply on the legitimacy of his campaigning activity. Obviously Nader presents something of a troublesome figure for *Nationwide*; on the one hand he claims to stand for the 'rights of the consumer' much in the way that *Nationwide* does, on the other hand his activities have a 'maverick' quality. But, even when Greene presses the point, invoking what 'many people' think:

> Greene: 'Would you be unhappy if you were described, as many people have described you, as an agitator?'

Nader is granted the space in his reply to redefine Greene's question and to answer it in his own terms:

> Nader: 'Well you see any change involves agitation, King George found this out two hundred years ago and . . . of course, by definition, any improvement requires a change of the prior status quo, or displacement of it, and so I think that's a very important role for people to play because there's a lot of change needed in our world today.'

(vii) Controlling the discourse: the work of nomination

'Tonight we meet the person who . . .' is a characteristic *Nationwide* introduction, but the point is that although we may 'meet' a host of individuals in the course of the programme, we never meet them direct. The 'meeting' is carefully set up by the *Nationwide* team. Thus, we are told in the regional menu that we will:

> TC (direct address) to camera: 'join the lady who was attacked by the lions in the Safari park as she goes back again to meet the lions.'

After the first section of local news we cut again to Tom Coyne in his role as outdoor linkman. He first supplies the textual link, situating this item in the flow of the programme:

> TC: 'Well there's going to be more news of course later in the programme.'

Then he moves on to introduce and frame this particular item, first linking it back to an earlier story covered by the programme:

> TC: 'I wonder if you remember this dramatic picture we showed you a few weeks ago of Mrs Barbara Carter of Halesowen. She was attacked by lions in the West Midlands Safari park. Well after an experience like that you'd hardly expect Mrs Carter to be keen on seeing lions again. But today she visited a farm near Stratford on Avon to do just that . . .'

Mrs Carter's status and identity as a newsworthy person are established; her actions are situated in our frame of expectations – the focus is placed on her doing something 'you'd hardly expect' – breaking the frame of our everyday expectations and therefore being newsworthy (cf., introduction to 'Americans in England': 'let's hear from another part of East Anglia, from Suffolk this time although you *might think* it was a bit of America.') Coyne then nominates the reporter for the story:

TC: 'A report from Alan Towers.'

At the end of the interview the newsreader moves momentarily out of his impartial role, to add a personal comment:

A much braver and a very determined person than I could ever be.

before moving on to the next story – a report of a policeman attempting to rescue a woman from a fire. At the end of that item the newsreader's comment links it back to Mrs Carter's story:

Two stories of bravery.

Similarly, the interview with Ralph Nader is introduced by a statement which clearly 'statuses' the interviewee:

Coyne (d/a to camera): 'You know America's leading campaigner on consumer affairs, Ralph Nader . . .'

followed by a framing/introductory question:

. . . we hear of you on all sorts of controversial topics . . . what motivates you to get into all these different fields?

The introduction and the question thus tell us Nader's status and competence and establish the topic on which he is to speak; again in the interview with Patrick Meehan we find the two stage introductory frame at work:

Barratt (d/a to camera): 'This afternoon, as you may have heard, Patrick Meehan was released from prison in Peterhead, so over now to David Scott in Aberdeen.'

Barratt thus nominates the reporter, who continues:

Scott (d/a to camera): 'Meehan was released from prison after seven years. Most of it had been spent in solitary confinement as a protest against his conviction . . .'

The chain of nomination passes from Barratt, as presenter, to the regional reporter, and only then to Meehan – his appearance is by no means a direct access or meeting with the audience: it has been 'framed', we have been told who he is, what is remarkable about him and how long ago (two hours) he got out of jail. His status for-the-programme is pre-established.

At the end of the interview Barratt (speaking d/a to camera again) sums up the item in a way that contextualises it and thus attempts to encode it within a preferred interpretation:

> Barratt: 'Patrick Meehan, who of course has served seven years of a life sentence for murder – a conviction based *yet again* on identification evidence' [his emphasis].

Here Barratt proposes a dominant framework for the interpretation of the events portrayed and retrospectively inserts the item into the frame; only he, as presenter, can authoritatively lay claim to the right to privilege one interpretation in this way. Meehan, on the other hand, can only speak *within* the frame set by the interviewer, which itself is within the frame set by the presenter.

Within the interview itself, *Nationwide* has a lesser degree of control over the discourse: thus Meehan repeatedly tries to 'break the frame' that has been set up for him – talking about the political issues behind the case rather than about his feelings while in prison:

> Meehan: '. . . I think it's wrong that, er, when things happen in places like America that people over here should become all sanctimonious and criticise, little do they know that the same things are happening here and the whole system is geared to prevent these things coming to the surface . . .'

Indeed, at the point where he claims that he was framed by British Intelligence *Nationwide* has to resort to the ultimate level of control (cutting the film) in order to maintain the dominant direction of the discourse.

Control, then, is not simply 'given' by the structure of the discourse; it has to be maintained, at times through an ongoing struggle, by specific discursive strategies, on the studio floor. In this interview Meehan repeatedly attempts to answer the questions that he would have liked to have been asked rather than those he is asked: that is, he attempts to gloss or inflect the discourse in his favour (cf., the 'yes, but . . .' strategy identified in Connell et al. 1976):

> . . . the first thing I want to do is pursue the matter further, er, for a public enquiry, and, er, I hope that within the next few days I'll be back in court applying . . . for permission to bring an action against, er, certain, witnesses shall we call them, for perjury.

The interviewer is then faced with the difficulty of steering the discussion back to the realms of feelings and personal experience:

69

You sound quite bitter . . .
What was your daily routine in prison?

In this interview, then, we see a struggle being conducted over the very terms of the discourse. This is not a struggle about what 'answers' are acceptable – since, strictly speaking, the interviewer cannot precisely prescribe what his respondent will say; and he cannot directly contradict, counter, or break off the interview after an 'unacceptable' reply without prejudicing or rupturing the protocol within which this type of interview operates. These interviews are based on an apparent equivalence between interviewer and respondent – equal parties to the conversation – and they are governed by the protocols which provide the 'rule' in all current affairs TV – the protocols of 'objectivity' (of the interviewer) and 'balance' (between interviewer and interviewee). But it *is* a struggle over the way items are framed – over which 'frame' is operating or dominant. The frame is the device which, though it cannot absolutely prescribe the content of a reply, does prescribe and delimit the *range* of 'acceptable' replies. It is an ideological strategy, in the precise sense that, when it works, it sustains a certain spontaneous circularity – the form of the answers being already presupposed in the form of the questions. It is also ideological in the sense that it sustains an apparent equality in the exchange, whilst being founded on an unequal relationship – since the respondent must reply to a question within a frame he/she does not construct.

In sustaining, through the exchange, the tendency to reply within this restricted limit, much depends on the 'rule' of acceptability: a reply must appear to be relevant to the question, while sustaining the sense of 'natural following-on', good conversational practice, flow, natural continuity. To make an 'unacceptable' reply, whilst maintaining coherence, relevance, continuity and flow, entails a very special kind of work – a struggle in conversational practice: first, to re-frame or re-phrase (e.g., to break the 'personal experience' frame, and to replace it with an alternative, 'political' frame); second, then to reply within the reconstituted framework. It is in this sense that interviewing and responding, within the dominant discursive strategies of this kind of programme, entail the work (for the presenters) of *securing* the dominant frame (for it cannot be taken for granted as unproblematically given), and sometimes also (for the respondents) of struggling against or countering the dominant frame (though these counter-positions are by no means always taken up.)

4 'A nation of families . . .'

Nationwide, in its regular weekday concern to bring its audience 'some of the more interesting stories of life in today's Britain', constantly 'makes new' the understanding of national individuality which is its premise. Heath and Skirrow argue:

> television is an apparatus used for the production-reproduction of the novelistic; it seems to address the problem of the definition of forms of individual meaning within the limits of existing social representations and their determining social relations, the provision and maintenance of terms of social intelligibility for the individual. (Heath and Skirrow 1977, p. 58.)

We are concerned here with the production of a specific televisual discourse:

> little dramas of making sense in which the viewer as subject is carried along – in which, indeed, the individual becomes 'the viewer', the point of view of the sense of the programme. (ibid.)

Nationwide's discourse is specific – both to the medium in which it is constituted (television) and to a specific area of discourse within television (topical current affairs). But it is also specific in terms of the field of 'existing social representations and their determining social relations' on which it draws. We attempt in this section to delineate this field. We attempt to provide here some of the grounds on which to argue that *Nationwide's* ideological specificity lies in its orchestration, through regions, of individuals (in their families – see below) into the *televisual* coherence of 'the nation now'. To risk a general characterisation of that kind may appear to run counter to the diverse content and aims of the programme. But this heterogeneity must be seen in relation to Barthes' comment in discussing 'Myth Today':

> To the quantitative abundance of the forms there corresponds a small number of concepts. (Barthes 1972, p. 120.)

In *Nationwide*, we would argue, the abundance of newsworthy items which the programme produces nightly 'corresponds' to a small number of core ideological concepts. That is, items are produced through, and overdetermined by, a particular set of understandings of the social world (and the viewer's and England's place in it) which we have attempted to specify (see chapter 2) as the programme's basic 'themes'.

(i) *Nationwide* at home: pictures of everyday life

If *Panorama* articulates the sphere of institutional politics, foreign policies and affairs of state, *Nationwide* by contrast clearly focuses away from the public, institutional world, onto the domestic sphere. The focus is on the realm of family life and 'leisure', the sphere of 'freedom' where individuals can express their individualities: the world of hobbies, of regional traditions and differences, the domain of everyday life.

This has led us to speak of the *Nationwide* discourse as articulated, above all, through the sphere of *domesticity*. Several different aspects of the programme are gathered under this designation of *Nationwide*'s principal ideological field. It relates to the programme's explicit focus on issues affecting 'family life'. In this respect, it is crucial to note that whereas *Panorama* or *This Week* treat individuals in their public-institutional social roles, *Nationwide* treats individuals as members of *families*. In the *Nationwide* discourse 'individuals' and 'families' are coterminous. This focus is reinforced by the programme's orientation to the 'family audience' as a target group, by its timing in the evening schedule for exactly that moment when individuals are reconstituted once again, from their different and varied tasks and occupations, into the 'unity' of the family scene. But domesticity also accounts for the programme's mode of presentation: its emphasis on the ordinary, everyday aspects of issues, on the effects of general issues and problems on particular individuals and families. It is sustained in the very jigsaw nature of the 'menu' of a typical *Nationwide* evening – 'something for everyone'; above all, in its preoccupation with topics of 'human interest', the infinite variety of ordinary life'. Domesticity also is sustained through the recurring cycle of familiar topics, through the *Titbits/Daily Mirror* style of reporting, through the 'everyday' angle of the questions posed, the 'bringing it all back to common sense' thrust of the items: the 'normalising' impetus. Even when *Nationwide* is not explicitly dealing with 'the family', its dominant mode of representation is defined through its domestication of the world.

Nationwide focuses here on 'what we all share' (or are assumed to share); in many respects the programme displays our regional and individual differences and heterogeneity, but the domestic field in which these items are routinely situated acts as a frame to these differences. There is a concern here for what we have in common, beyond the level of our individual differences: the family home and its problems. This concern is evidenced at many levels (choice of items, style of treatment, etc.), but is also given an interesting stress by the programme's main figurehead and anchorman during the period of our viewing, Michael Barratt.

In his autobiography Barratt stresses the importance of family life; not only how his job interferes with it, but also how he dashed back from Berlin to be with the 'wife and kids' on Christmas Eve. Just as Barratt stresses them here, *Nationwide* observes the rituals of the domestic calendar: Christmas, Shrove Tuesday, Bank Holidays, etc. Also, for *Nationwide* fame is no substitute for the joys of family life, clearly; in the programme people who have achieved 'success' but are without friends and family ('the rich man who doesn't want any friends', 'the hermit of the Cotswolds' (1/6/76)) are portrayed as either unhappy or eccentric.

Barratt negotiates the difficult situation of being 'just an ordinary family man' and being famous too, by defining his priorities clearly with the former.

After describing various travels, exciting adventures, meetings with Zsa Zsa Gabor and Albert Schweitzer, he writes:

> And outside the studio, how good is the good life? The posh restaurants and the plush hotels. The fast cars, the fat cheques. Another myth. I enjoy eating out with Joan or with close friends (who are more likely to be country men than 'personalities') in restaurants not too far from home, preferably where it is not necessary to wear a jacket or tie. Cod and chips out of paper is my delight. Its only rival is roast lamb at home for Sunday lunch. (Barratt 1973, p. 27.)

Like Michael Barratt, *Nationwide* is 'at home' even when it appears to be 'out in the world'. 'Home' is the – sometimes marked, sometimes unmarked, but always 'present' – centre of the *Nationwide* world. In this sense, the whole of *Nationwide*'s discourse is predicated on a particular way of structuring the world, and on the complex matrix of imagery and social relations through which this structure is sustained. It depends, essentially, on the contrasting couple of the world/the home and thus it is predicated, however invisibly (in terms of the manifest references of the programme), on the sexual division of labour, which

> ... under capitalism takes the extreme form of separation of the general economic process into a domestic and an industrial unit. (Coulson, Magas and Wainwright 1975, p. 60.)

Behind the taken-for-granted form of this separation of social life into two distinct, contrasted 'spheres', there lies the long historical process through which the household has gradually been separated (as a distinct world of its own) from the relations of production and exchange, its transformation into a private sphere, concerned exclusively with the essential functions of maintaining and reproducing the labourer and his family. (Cf., Engels 1975, Zaretsky 1976.) This separation has been accompanied by, and constructed through, the development of what were, originally, class specific ideologies of domesticity, of personal and family life (Davidoff 1976, C. Hall 1974). The 'domestic' world has been signified, ideologically, as the sphere which is separated and protected from the nasty business of making, doing and producing. It is where 'people' are produced; it is thus also where 'people' can be most 'themselves'. It is not only where we become 'individuals' but the domain in which we can most fully and satisfyingly express our individuality. The domain of domesticity thus has the effect of abstracting individuals from the network of social relations 'outside', and of reconstituting them into the unity of the family, the domestic. Against the divisions, distinctions and complexities of 'the outside' is set this privileged centre of familiar relations, which becomes, even in its literal absence, the measure of all that is worthwhile.

This 'domestication' of the world can be related to more general ideological effects; Hall, for example, has argued that:

One way of thinking the general function of ideology . . . is in terms of what Poulantzas (1975) calls 'separation' and 'uniting'. In the sphere of market relations and of 'egoistic private interest' (the sphere preeminently of civil society) the productive classes appear or are represented as (a) individual economic units driven by private and egoistic interests alone, which are (b) bound by the multitude of invisible contracts – the 'hidden hand' of capitalist exchange relations . . . this representation has the effect, first, of shifting emphasis from production to exchange, second of fragmenting classes into individuals, third of binding individuals into that 'passive community' of consumers. Likewise, in the sphere of the state and of juridico-political ideology, the political classes and class relations are represented as individual subjects (citizens, the voter, the sovereign individual in the eyes of the law and the representative system, etc.) and these individual political-legal subjects are then 'bound together' as members of a nation, united by the 'social contract', and by their common and mutual 'general interest'. Once again, the class nature of the State is masked: classes are redistributed into individual subjects: and these individuals are united within the imaginary coherence of the State, the nation and the national interest. (Hall 1977, pp. 336–37.)

Connell et al. (1977, p. 116) point out that it is wrong to imagine that the agents of production appear as individuals only in superstructural relations and not within the structure of the relations of production itself. The individualisation of agents really occurs in the process of the exchange of commodities, and in the sale of labour power as a commodity.

Out of the act of exchange itself, the individual, each one of them, is reflected in himself as its exclusive and dominant (determinant) subject . . . (Marx 1973, pp. 244–5.)

The point here is that the 'noisy sphere' of exchange relations in the market

provides the basis for those superstructural practices and ideological forms in which men are forced to 'live an imaginary relation' of equivalence and individualism to their real (non-equivalent, collective) conditions of existence . . . [Civil Society] is no longer the seat and source of individualism. It is simply the individualising sphere of the circuit of capital's path to expanded reproduction. Individualism is not the origin of the system . . . it is what capital produces as one of its necessary phenomenal forms – one of its necessary but dependent effects. (Hall, Lumley, McLellan 1977, p. 62.)

'Individualism' is, therefore, sited within those social relations which are specific to the relations of exchange and consumption. In our culture, the individual is, therefore, given a special, privileged position in the relations of civil society (the sphere, classically, of 'egoistic impulses and exchange'), and in the relations and ideologies which fill out and sustain the juridical (the 'legal subject', equal to all other subjects in the eyes of the law) and the political domains (the 'political subject', equally represented with all other citizens). But the attention to the juridical and political aspects has tended to disguise and mask the equally important source and foundation of the ideologies of 'individualism' in the domestic and familial sphere.

(ii) Labourers in their private lives

The reproduction and maintenance of the working class, which as Marx argues is a precondition of the reproduction of capital (Marx 1961, p. 572), has historically taken place in the family, and been the concern primarily of women. Increasing state intervention has left women morally responsible for this work, although some of its burden (differently at different periods; CSE 1975, Wilson 1977) has been shifted from paid to unpaid work, and the penetration of the home by commodities has transformed its nature. It is, historically, in the family that the individual who engages in the act of exchange as 'its exclusive and dominant (determinant) subject' is reproduced and maintained.

The home, as a separate and 'naturalised' sphere, apparently undetermined by the mode of production, is itself structured by the labourer's relation to the moment of exchange in which he

> manages both to alienate his labour power and to avoid renouncing his rights of ownership over it. (Marx 1976, p. 717.)

This structure effects a crucial separation:

> The worker's productive consumption and his individual consumption are therefore totally distinct. In the former, he acts as the motive power of capital, and belongs to the capitalist. In the latter, he belongs to himself, and performs his necessary vital functions outside the production process. (Marx 1976, p. 717.)

It is in this 'private sphere', structured through the sexual division of labour, where individuals are interpellated as sexed subjects, that individuality is understood to express itself outside the determinations of the mode of production and juridico-political constraints. Perceived as outside 'the system', the family, as site of the material practices of procreation and the maintenance and reproduction of the labour force, is also the site of the most elaborated articulation of the ideology of 'individualism' as 'origin of the system'.

Thus the increasingly elaborated distinctions between 'home' and 'work' (which have contributed to the invisibility of work done by women in the home), have to be understood at a theoretical level in relation to both the reproduction of capital and women's subordination.

Zaretsky summarises the historical process as one whereby:

> Work, in the form of wage labour, was removed from the centre of family life, to become the means by which family life was maintained. Society divided and the family became the realm of 'private life'. . . (Zaretsky 1976, p. 57.) 'Work' and 'life' were separated; proletarianisation split off the outer world of alienated labour from an inner world of personal feeling . . . it created a separate sphere of personal life, seemingly divorced from the mode of production. (Ibid., p. 30.)

The workings and ideological articulation of this separate sphere cannot be understood without attention to women's special place within it. There is a type of collapse; the woman somehow is the home, the woman and the home seem to become each other's attributes. Thus Ruskin's famous description in 1868:

> This is the true nature of home, it is the place of peace; the shelter, not only from all injury, but from all terror, doubt and division . . . So far as the anxieties of the outer life penetrate into it . . . it ceases to be a home; it is then only a part of the outer world which you have roofed over and lighted a fire in . . . *And whenever a true wife comes, this home is always round her.* (Quoted in Millett 1971, pp. 98–9. Our emphasis.)

This is an image from a masculine point of view:

> The underlying imagery is the unacknowledged master of the household, looking in, so to speak, at the household he has 'created'. The 'domestic interior' awaits his coming, his return. (Davidoff, L'Esperance, Newby 1976, p. 159.)

This image is premised on an understanding of women as being 'themselves' exclusively when they are 'wives and mothers': that is, it is an image predicated on their socio-economic inequality and dependence, as well as on their psycho-sexual subordination (Comer 1973). Historically, this 'image' first became the dominant one within the bourgeois household; but it has been generalised outside the bourgeois family, extended to many women who, though they may well now be wage-workers themselves, nevertheless subscribe to it as 'norm' and 'ideal'. Few women 'live' this ideology without some deep sense of its contradictions – the so-called 'rewards' of being 'special' as wives and mothers constantly co-existing with the reality of their isolation, exploitation and subordination. But, in so far as this variant of the 'familial' ideology remains the dominant one, it serves to perpetuate and sustain the oppression of women, both inside and outside the home:

Consciously or unconsciously, the world has been conceived in the image of the bourgeois family – the husband is the breadwinner and the wife remains at home attending to housework and childcare. Both the household itself and women's domestic labour within it are presented as the unchanging backcloth to the world of real historical activity. (Alexander 1976, p. 59.)

Davidoff, L'Esperance and Newby argue:

In their suburban homes, wives are still expected to create a miniature version of the domestic idyll, set in subtopian pseudo-rural estate surroundings while their male counterparts swarm into central city offices and factories. Wives remain protectors of the true community, the 'still point'; a basic moral force to which the workers, travellers and seekers can return. In the archetypal portrayal of everyday life they still wait, albeit with less resignation as well as less hope, for the hand upon the latch. (p. 175.)

This is the image of the home upon which *Nationwide* bases (and times) itself. The family home is 'provided' for, in material terms, through the waged work of men and women: it is maintained as an economic unit through women's unwaged work, through their continuing subordination. Without these material supports, it would not exist. Yet in its archetypal portrayal as the centre of 'everyday life', it is re-presented as the refuge from the world of material constraints, the true measure of individuality, and thus as the last repository of essential 'human values' elsewhere crushed by the forces and pressures of 'modern life'. *Nationwide* rarely deals with the first but it constantly traffics in the second of these aspects: thus it constantly articulates the real relations of the social and sexual division of labour through this displacement into the space of the 'domestic'. In this space – and the realms of leisure and recreation, hobbies and personal tastes, consumption and 'personal relations' which especially belong to it and fill it out as a 'lived' domain – people (especially men) can exercise that 'freedom' denied them within the sphere of alienated labour. This is *Nationwide*'s primary sphere of operation: 'reflecting' the activities of the individuals and families which comprise the nation, in their personal capacities: in their domestic lives.

Nationwide's discourse is, then, founded on a very specific mode of representing individuals and families which is so taken-for-granted within the programme that it requires to be made explicit here, making visible what *Nationwide* makes invisible, but constantly assumes. It is through these assumptions that *Nationwide* produces and reproduces, in its selection and presentation of items, a particular image of England, which is unremittingly grounded in its own obviousness ('Many people would say . . .'), in the construction of which its audience is both constitutive and constituted. The stream of 'subjects' interviewed gives authenticity to this 'real world of people', which then appears as the 'guarantee' of its reality – as does the audience itself – through both its implication and participation in, for example, such exercises as the *Nationwide* slimming campaign.

In an attempt to delineate the connotative image of England through which the nation is constructed, we produced a sentence in which we seemed able to locate the whole range of *Nationwide* items, in a way which allowed some ordering of the connotations in which the programme deals. In a modified form, this sentence also underlies the categorisation of items we have used:

ENGLAND, A COUNTRY WHICH IS ALSO A NATION, IN THE MODERN WORLD,

Regions	of Families	Technological Advance
Localism	of Individuals	Fast-moving
Town and		Alienating
Country		

WITH OUR OWN SPECIAL HERITAGE AND . . . PROBLEMS

Traditions	Bureaucracy
Calendar	Prices
Eccentricities	Unions
Patriotism	Balance of Payments

(iii) Regionalism and nationalism *Nationwide*

Within the discourse of *Nationwide* the concept of the nation is not presented as a monolithic entity, immediately embracing us all – rather the unity of the nation is constructed out of the sum of our regional differences and variations. As argued earlier, *Nationwide*'s history was specifically informed by the attempt to break away from the idea of a blanket metropolitan dominance and bias; indeed the 'life of the regions' is a crucial ingredient in the *Nationwide* formula, as well as being integral to how the programme is constructed technically.

Over a long period Britain has experienced a tendency towards the destruction of regional differentiation – the result of many factors, including the effects of the educational system, and of television itself. At the present time, however, there is of course a countervailing movement towards regional separatism, manifested in the 'nationalism' of Wales and Scotland, the revival of the movement towards national independence in Northern Ireland, and some forms of regional devolution. When *Nationwide* was first established it had enough on its plate to rake up the dying embers of 'regional' consciousness, but this is now doubly problematic. Firstly because of the weakening of English regionalism, and secondly, ironically, because of the vitality of a regional 'awakening' on the Celtic fringes. In the present context *Nationwide* has both to rub the lamp to conjure up the dead spirits in the counties, and to try and control the wild spirits beyond them.

Within this context, the programme adopts a range of different strategies:

on the one hand, *Nationwide* through its reporters (who are themselves established as having their own close regional links) can bring the news of the regions' activities to the attention of the nation: reporting the activities of the peripheries to the metropolis. But the stress is also on bringing you 'your own news and programmes from your own corner of England', local news for a local audience, concretising national issues by dealing with them as they appear 'on your doorstep'; e.g., in 'Midlands Today', dealing with a national issue (the future of British Leyland) as it affects the immediate prospects of the local workforce. Alternatively, issues of immediate local concern can be presented as important news (the future of a well known local building), or local issues can be given national status (e.g., the lions of Cradley Heath achieve national notoriety; Princess Anne opens a local hospital).

The *Nationwide* enactment of 'regionality' then, involves both:

(1) The invention of regional differentiation via *Nationwide*'s own internal processes of regional cultural manufacture; e.g., *Nationwide* events like the boat-race in which each region had its own yacht.

(2) The adoption and transformation of real differences between the regions; e.g., Mike Neville's continuous play on Geordie 'sub culture', which is made into the symbolic/representative dialect and stock-in-trade for the whole of the North-East, although in reality it is only a feature of a particular part.

The 'regional' character of *Nationwide* is clearly pivotal to its identity, to what makes the programme distinctive. The way the items are put together into a unified programme has a great deal to do with the way it is articulated between the two poles – 'region' and 'nationwide'. It is as if the programme, first, locates 'you' in your local-regional place; and, from that point of identification, it can survey for you (enable you to construct) a view of the nation as a whole – nationwide. These axes are clearly evident in the very way the programme is billed in the *Radio Times*. (See chapter 1.) The national scene is usually presented as seen from the vantage point of 'your corner of England'. If *Nationwide* constructs the 'nation' as a representative or imaginary whole, it does so through the construction of regional viewpoints. This articulation is then, of course, constantly realised in the programme itself, which not only combines regional news (different for and specific to each region) with national news, but also, in its feature items, constantly stresses the 'regional' origin of particular items, or nominates a topic and then takes a 'round-up' of regional views, reactions, experiences. If the principal anchoring role is that provided by the central figure in the London studio (in our viewing period, Michael Barratt), the programme nevertheless is constantly 'going out' to the regions from this point and 'returning' to home base: the 'nation' is always 'dropping in' on the regions. One of the favourite visual shots peculiar to *Nationwide* is Barratt shown facing the bank of screens, each with a 'regional' presenter's face, all 'regionally' available to him, to be called on, each piped in (as the *mandala* represents, graphically) from the regional corners of England to 'the centre'. Without this complex set of oscillations – centre/periphery, region/nation – *Nationwide* could not adequately construct that representation of what 'the nation' consists of, a representation which is – in the whole range of current affairs programmes on all channels – quite peculiarly specific to it.

If we ask, what is the ideological effect of constructing 'the nation' in this way, we would suggest that it is a representation which constructs England as a complex of regionalisms, as an entity marked principally by its spatial 'unity-in-difference'. These regional differences and variations do not, within the discourse of the programme, conflict with one another, cancel or contradict one another. In the 'hard news' items the growing problem of regional economic underdevelopment sometimes surfaces. But it is not a pertinent theme in the items which *Nationwide* characteristically generates for itself. In the latter parts of the programme, the differences are each to be savoured and enjoyed for their own peculiarities and distinctive flavours; the nation is the sum of these distinctive regional characteristics. The nation becomes 'one' by the simple addition of all the regions – a form of unity through juxtaposition. This represents England as a nation which is a complex but non-contradictory unity.

Nationwide's regions are almost exclusively *cultural*. It is their cultural traditions, peculiarities, characteristics, distinctive identities which establish them, all equally 'English' in their difference. The regionalism of the programme therefore forges close connections with the whole domain of tradition – regional crafts, pastimes, etc. – which is discussed in the following section. But it can be said here that the culture of regionalism on *Nationwide* is massively linked with the *rural* aspects of regional life (cf., chapter 2.iii(d)) and hence with the 'past', and with a kind of cultural nostalgia for 'old folkways, values and customs', which it is *Nationwide*'s privilege to rediscover and indeed celebrate, against all the other 'modern' tendencies which are fast obliterating these critical cultural differences.

But the regions are also 'regional' in a technical sense; i.e., the BBC is 'regionalised' by its transmitting grid, which is in turn determined by technical factors: the siting of transmitters, boosters and studios. The cultural and common sense map of regional identities which segments the world of *Nationwide* is, in fact, based on and supported by a technical and material system. And it is the technical links between regional centres of television production, across the country, which enables *Nationwide* to operate 'region-ally' – a fact which dictates many aspects of the visual forms of the programme, and of its organisational features (drawing more widely than any other single TV programme on the BBC's regional news and feature facilities). There is a 'regional' staff employed on *Nationwide* in each of the major regions. In Birmingham, for example, the technical staff and apparatus for the region's contribution includes three cameras and cameramen, a floor manager, one or two scene hands, a producer, producer's assistant/secretary and a director.

Each region is responsible for its own *Nationwide* budget. There are *Nationwide* researchers attached to each region to scan the area for possible feature items. In addition to the great concentration of resources and manpower needed to sustain *Nationwide* at its nerve centre in London, there are smaller *Nationwide* units replicated throughout the broadcasting regions. Technically, however, London is very much in control. There are three systems for locking in, *Nationwide*:

General Lock: Regions – London
National Lock: London – Regions
ICE Lock: London – Regions (Insertion Communications Equipment)

This latter form of the lock is that which combines regional inputs to the programme with London through the device of Colour Separation Overlay (see below).

The regional-centre articulation of the programme, based on these complex forms of technical coupling, requires very careful synchronisation between London and the regions. This includes – apart from extremely careful timing (as the programme moves between regions/centre especially in the opening parts) – matching of line, frame and colour phase. The regions are connected to London by GPO land cable. When London receives a 'message' from a region, it has to transmit back information about the degree of matching, to enable the correct adjustments to be made (line, frame, colour). This 'information' is in fact carried in the top seven lines of the TV image, which each region magnifies in order to decode and adjust accordingly. Hence, there are complex and specialised technical means which enable the shifts and transitions – region-to-'nation' – to be made *naturally* – i.e., without the viewer registering the shifts through manifest lacks of synchronisation.

One of the most widely used techniques in *Nationwide* is Colour Separation Overlay. This enables an image from one region to be 'overlaid' on to a space in the frame from another region, so that two images with different regional sources appear, not only within a single frame, but with both images on a single plane. This is achieved by placing the subject to be isolated against a blue backdrop; this backdrop will not be registered by the master camera, thus leaving a space in the picture which is filled by an image from a second camera. This second camera can, of course, be piping the second image down the line from another region. The effect of CSO will be to combine these two images into a single composite picture. Thus – though this is not usually allowed by the BBC's professional code – the transmitted picture could be made to signify that two people, who were in fact in different rooms, miles away from each other, were sitting in the same room, having a conversation. The use of CSO in *Nationwide* therefore not only considerably extends the degree to which different regional images can be 'composited', but also sustains the illusion of the many 'natural' links which bind the regions together.

The unity which composes the nation in *Nationwide*'s terms may be said to find some homology of structure with the character of the links between items, discussed earlier. It is implicit in the *Nationwide* representation of 'the nation' that the programme must constantly move, not only from one sort of item to a very different one (one of its main virtues being its variety, its heterogeneity) but also from one place to another. As we have argued, this heterogeneity has to be woven into a coherent programme: the distinctive *Nationwide* 'mix' of items, usually signalled at the start of the programme by the giving of the evening's 'menu' of items and the links which create smooth transitions between wildly different items and themes. But, like the 'nation' which the sum of these items constructs, this unity of approach is of an 'open' kind – allowing the different items, stories and places to *coexist*. Hence, the 'menu' is usually permissive rather than directive and obligatory, stressing variety rather than imposing a strict hierarchy of stories. Accordingly, the connections signalled in the 'menus' are loose connections, conjunctural in form: 'and another thing . . .' The discourse of the typical *Nationwide* menu stresses the element of *contingency* – as if it just happens, by chance, that this evening's dip into what the editor of the *Daily Mirror*, Hugh Cudlipp, once called 'the rich, full bran-tub of life' produces this miscellany of interesting things: each different from the other, each in its own way as interesting as the other.

The power of the *Nationwide* presentation, then, derives from, and is relayed through, its localised, concretised character; moreover, it is relayed through a further identification with the localised audience. In contrast to other, metropolitan-dominated current affairs programmes, *Nationwide* reporters and presenters will often speak in the regional dialect of their area. The programme celebrates its televisual regionalism; thus the play on regional pronunciations:

The River Ure? The Yer. The Yure? The Yerr. (*Nationwide* from East Anglia, 19/5/76.)

Significantly the *Nationwide* reporter on the item covering the anniversary of the Jarrow hunger march was accredited as 'knowing' the particular area of Lancashire which the march had reached at that point: being familiar with those local conditions and therefore qualified to 'report it back' to the centre. This is a crucial condition of *Nationwide*'s sphere of operations. The issues are concretised, localised by familiar place-name tags: indeed they are formulated as local/regional issues. John Downing (1976) argues that this kind of localised presentation is particularly powerful precisely in so far as it works by grounding itself in the reproduction of familiar concrete sense-impressions, thus reproducing and reinforcing the spontaneous forms of localised, sectional class-consciousness. (Cf., Beynon 1976; Lane 1974; Nicholls and Armstrong 1976 on factory class consciousness.)

It has recently been argued that in the case of a 'populist' TV series, such as *The Sweeney*, there is a crucial emphasis on making this kind of 'identification' with the programme's audience both at the level of vocabulary, where:

the use of a certain kind of demotic speech . . . defines the programme as being 'of the people' if not exactly working class . . .'

and at the visual level where the programme:

uses not the tourists' London of Big Ben and Buckingham Palace, but the London 'of the people': Ladbroke Grove, the docks, Shepherd's Bush . . . (Buscombe 1976, p. 68.)

While *Nationwide* speaks more clearly to a petit bourgeois (and older) audience than does *The Sweeney*, the programme's project is aimed in a parallel direction: to present a 'popular' perspective, to speak in the 'language of the people', through the code of localised/regional presentation. In adopting the forms of regional speech the programme lays claim to 'our/insiders'' local-authoritative knowledge and understanding of events.

(iv) The myth of the nation

Fragmentation by regional difference is, however, framed in *Nationwide* by the idea of our 'special national heritage': a tradition and a set of values which we are all as individuals assumed to share.

This material is focused in the 'country' and 'conservationist' range of *Nationwide*'s repertoire (see chapter 2.iii(d)). Here *Nationwide*'s regional/populist orientation picks up on the activities of revivalists concerned with maintaining 'traditional' customs and institutions, or the programme itself performs this function, searching out surviving practitioners of older crafts 'in your corner of England'. As Raymond Williams points out:

All traditions are selective; the pastoral tradition quite as much as any other. (Williams 1976, p. 28.)

Nationwide situates 'the tradition', a national heritage of customs and values, threatened and eroded by modern industrial society, in an image of England dominated by the 'rural past'. What is elided here is both the class basis of 'traditional culture' as it existed historically – it is simply 'our tradition', as members of the nation – and the political content of that culture as it exists today. (Cf., Lloyd 1969 on 'traditional' culture in an urban industrial setting.)

This, then, is an always-already nostalgic perspective on a tradition rooted in the past – but *Nationwide* also clearly marks out the value of progress. Some aspects of the past we are well rid of; fundamental among these is the notion of class, which is situated as belonging to the 'bad old days'. In its presentation of the anniversary of the Jarrow march *Nationwide* displayed a double inflection of the material. On the one hand the events were translated out of their foundation in a specific class history and experience; the march was presented as the 'plight' of a town or region, not of a class or a system. Here 'regionality' becomes a code of social organisation through which class forces are represented. But, secondly, the very class structure was situated in the past in an image of the 'Northern Community' which itself belongs to the past – the days of the futile slogans of a cloth-cap, class-conscious nineteenth century social-ism. (*Nationwide* 22/3/73.)

Interestingly, Nicholls and Armstrong found a similar 'blurring' of categories among some of the foremen in their 'Chemco' plant – who, they noted were

> given to use any of the terms 'the North', 'the working class', or 'the past' as a shorthand for the others. (Nicholls and Armstrong 1976, p. 130.)

This 'blurring' is precisely significant in its negotiation of a contradictory image of the trade union movement, which *Nationwide* also shares; the unions are seen to have a positive social role ('a lot of people would agree you're in need of more money' – Barratt to striking trade union representative, *Nationwide* 13/3/73), coexisting uneasily with a negative industrial role ('They do seem rather daft reasons for going on strike . . .' – Barratt, *Nationwide* 14/3/73). This contradiction is characteristic of the form of sectional/negotiated consciousness outlined by Parkin (1972, chapter 3), which frequently includes both accommodation and oppositional elements. But in *Nationwide* the contradiction is elided by situating the positive role of the unions *in the past:*

> because the 'social' good was achieved in the past, whereas the 'industrial' harm is taking place in the present . . . however necessary past struggles may have been, social justice [has] now been more or less achieved. To go on, as some militants want to, would be to go too far. (Nicholls and Armstrong 1976, p. 182.)

The image of 'nowadays' which is constructed in opposition to this image of the past is one which contains diversity but not structural difference; communities and regions are present in the discourse but classes, except in the past, are absent. If the 'contradictory unity' in which *Panorama* traffics is the construction of the 'idea of general interest', *Nationwide* is clearly operating some 'idea of the nation and its regions' as its imaginary coherence.

In the discourse of *Nationwide* the social structure of the nation is denied; spatial difference replaces social structure and the nation is seen to be composed not of social units in any relation of exploitation or antagonism but of geographical units often reduced to regional stereotypes or 'characters'.

This recomposition of the nation, from a set of elements that have been displaced out of their structural relations with one another, is performed, then, at what Roland Barthes would describe as a 'mythical' level, as in his analysis of the treatment of Paris:

> . . . the displaced parts are then rearranged into a mythical meta-language. Thus the swirling lights around the Arc de Triomphe, displaced from the real relations of Paris, the historico-commercial city,

are then, as 'empty but spectacular forms', reorganised, in a second system or meta-language, into the 'myth of the city at night . . .' (Barthes 1972.)

What the discourse of *Nationwide* produces, from the elements which have been displaced out of their structural relations with each other, is a myth of 'the nation, now'.

(v) It's only common sense

Nationwide, we have argued, is a programme of common sense, speaking to and from the 'ordinary viewer'. Thus, Barratt:

> I can do any programme they ask me to do because I ask the naïve questions that everyone wants the answers to. (*Daily Mirror* 11/7/77.)

We may usefully follow Nowell-Smith (1974) in distinguishing two meanings in the 'inherently ambiguous' concept of common sense:
(1) A form of pragmatic reasoning based on direct perception of the world and opposed to all forms of thought that lack this direct link with experience.
(2) Whatever understanding of the world happens to be generally held.
We would argue that common sense in both these meanings can be found to both construct and constitute this programme at several levels. Firstly we would suggest that Nowell-Smith's first sense can be used to approach both the verbal and visual discourse of the programme. To suggest that the programme's visual discourse is 'common-sensical' is obviously to draw heavily on, and summarise very crudely, a great deal of the work on realism and transparency in the cinema produced in recent years in *Screen* and elsewhere.

We have not established this here in a fuller analysis of the visual discourse. However, we would suggest that the programme relies on a practice and an ideology of television as a medium which allows a 'direct perception of the world', and provides an immediate and direct 'link with experience'. The programme's own productive work is rendered invisible.

The signification of a great many of the visual images of *Nationwide* is not, as Barthes described the photograph, in its 'having-been-there', (cf. Hall 1972: 'The Determinations of News Photographs') but rather, the 'being-thereness' of the reporter, interviewee or participants. Thus Michael Barratt writes, distinguishing between newspaper and television journalism:

> for television, you have to produce evidence of being on the spot. (Barratt 1973, p. 110.)

So in the 19 May programme, in the 'lady with the lion' sequence, Honeybunch's 'camera nerves' are commented on when she paws the camera lens, but this 'interruption' in transparency precisely guarantees the actuality of the report. The most complex articulation of this 'common-sense' about television is found in the regional 'link-up', where the technology which allows simultaneous images to be transmitted from the different regions is positively celebrated – the bank of screens appears – but celebrated as a technology which allows a direct-link with the experience of the regions.

We have already commented to some extent on *Nationwide*'s common-sense verbal discourse, and examined the way in which it interrelates with Nowell-Smith's second meaning: 'whatever understanding of the world happens to be generally held.' In relation to this second definition, we would argue that *Nationwide* constructs a particular 'understanding of the world' which is both specific to the programme and its production of 'the nation, nationwide', but which also draws on, and is read in the context of, already existing social representations. This production (connotatively paralleled in some ways in local newspapers and Radio 4) is distinguished by its dissolution of contradiction into difference and diversity, and self-legitimating in its populism, its claim to be the 'understanding of the world that is generally held'. *Nationwide*'s cast of thousands signifies thousands of individual endorsements of the generality of this 'world view', the contours of which we have already attempted to sketch in chapter 2. We now need to relate these common-sense effects in the *Nationwide* discourse more directly to the ideological work of *Nationwide* as a programme.

Althusser describes the elementary ideological effect as that of 'obviousness' (Althusser 1971, p. 161), and it is in relation to this conceptualisation of ideology that the ahistoricity, the naturalness, of common sense, should be considered. The immediate obviousness of common sense, its in-built rationale of reference to 'the real', its structure of *recognition*, forecloses historical and structural examination of its conclusions. The instant reference which contemporary common sense makes to a massively present and unalterable reality – simply, what is there, what everybody knows – denies both its own history and its specific content, the *bricolage* of more developed and sometimes archaic ideological systems which inform its empiricism (Gramsci 1968, Nowell-Smith 1974). Stuart Hall comments that common sense *feels* 'as if it has always been there, the sedimented, bedrock wisdom of "the race", a form of "natural" wisdom, the content of which has changed hardly at all with time'. He continues:

> You cannot learn, through common sense, how things are; you can only discover *where they fit* into the existing scheme of things. In this way, its very taken-for-grantedness is what establishes it as a medium in which its own premises and presuppositions are being rendered invisible by its apparent transparency. (Hall 1977, pp. 325–6.)

As noted earlier (chapter 1.iv) *Nationwide*'s verbal discourse is always constructed *as* the 'ordinary language' of its audience. The programme speaks in terms which have a resonance in popular thinking, utilising particularly in its 'links' the forms of everyday speech and popular 'wisdom':

orally transmitted tags, enshrining generalisations, prejudices and half-truths, elevated by epigrammatic phrasing into the status of maxims. (Hoggart 1957, p. 103.)

This 'common-sense' perspective of the programme has a particular force. In it 'feeling', 'personal experience' and immediate empirical perception are dominant; it is grounded in 'the personal and the concrete'; in particular, in local experiences. It is practical, opposed to abstraction and theorising; it

identifies the exact cause, simple and to hand, and does not let itself be distracted by fancy quibbles and pseudo-profound, pseudo-scientific metaphysical mumbo-jumbo. (Gramsci 1971, p. 348.)

Through its televisual common sense, 'based on direct perception of the world', the programme offers a direct picture of 'how things seem' Nationwide, and how the people involved in events feel about them. Nationwide's common sense must be understood in relation to the adequacy of common-sense explanations as lived:

Common sense is neither straightforwardly the class ideology of the bourgeoisie nor the spontaneous thinking of the masses. It is the way a subordinate class in class society lives its subordination. It is the acceptance by the subordinate class of the reality of class society, as seen from below. (Nowell-Smith 1974.)

Williams argues that common sense must be understood in relation to the concept of hegemony:

Hegemony . . . is also different from ideology in that it is seen to depend for its hold not only on its expression of the interests of a ruling class, but also its acceptance as 'normal reality' or 'common sense' by those in practice subordinated to it. (Williams 1975, p. 118.)

Common sense must be related to another aspect of hegemony:

It is a set of meanings and values which as they are experienced as practices appear as reciprocally confirming. (Williams 1973, p. 9.)

This 'reciprocal confirmation' points to, at one level, the 'undeniableness' of common-sense ideas. They must have, as Mepham argues:

a sufficient degree of effectiveness both in rendering social reality intelligible and in guiding practice within it for them to be apparently acceptable. (Mepham 1974, p. 100.)

In our view 'hegemony' cannot be understood solely in terms of class (or class fractions). As we have argued earlier, we are concerned in *Nationwide* with an image of the home constructed in masculine hegemony. The 'naturalness' of common sense cannot be separated from the common-sensical definition of women through their 'natural' and 'timeless' roles of wife and mother, roles which correspondingly define them as the 'bearers' and repository of a basic/natural wisdom, which is founded on their taken-for-granted separation from political life. Mattelart (1975) raises interesting points about the way in which the Chilean Right was precisely able to exploit the activity of women against the Allende regime by presenting their demonstrations

> as the spontaneous reaction of the most a-political sector of public opinion, brought together and activated by a natural survival instinct . . . behind demands which appeared unrelated to class strategy because they encompassed areas traditionally marginalised from the political sphere such as the home, family organisation . . . (Mattelart 1975, p. 19.)

We thus confront in *Nationwide* the contradictory nature of common sense. Its very strength, its concrete, particular character also constitute a crucial ideological limit; the always-local, concretised form of presentation of issues in the discourse of *Nationwide* precisely excludes the awareness of wider structural factors. As Harris argues of British Conservatism:

> The particular is its own justification, justified by its own existence (it *is* the real). (Harris 1971, p. 128.)

We are provided with an understanding of the world which is always:

> more or less limited and provincial, which is fossilised and anachronistic . . . corporate or economistic. (Gramsci 1971, p. 325.)

From this perspective it is impossible to grasp either the social formation as a whole or the role, for instance, of 'political' institutions, or of the sexual division of labour within this complex whole. Gramsci characterises aspects of this type of 'understanding' as a 'negative' class response in speaking of the peasantry, where:

> Not only does that people have no precise consciousness of its own historical identity, it is not even conscious of the . . . exact limits of its adversary. There is a dislike of 'officialdom', the only form in which the State is perceived. (Gramsci 1971, pp. 272–3.)

This is precisely the level at which the State is presented on *Nationwide*. The State 'appears' as the unwelcome intrusion of officialdom and bureaucracy, infringing on private freedoms. We are advised by the presenters on how to deal with the demands of this bureaucracy (advice on breathaliser laws, etc.); similarly the presenters represent us against the bureaucracy, against the inefficient gas board or local authority. What the discourse of *Nationwide* excludes is any awareness of dominance or subordination in relationships of class, race and gender. Politics is not presented in terms of power and control but in terms of bureaucracy, inefficiency, interference with the individual's rights.

Nationwide's characteristic style of presentation is to deal with 'issues' through 'individuals', dealing with an individual example of a problem, concentrating on the level of individual experience and felt 'effects'. Through this style of presentation the programme contracts a relationship with forms of common-sense thought which have deep roots in our spontaneous experience of society.

> Precisely, common sense does not require reasoning argument, logic, thought; it is spontaneously available, thoroughly recognisable, widely shared. (Hall 1977, p. 325.)

Moreover this perspective has a profound 'purchase' on the 'facts of common sense', precisely because these 'facts' have a certain validity in experience as a mirror of the way society really operates.

The *Nationwide* presentation, then, is concerned with immediacy, reflection; presenting pictures of 'the nation now'. *Nationwide*'s discourse always moves within the limits of what Marx described as 'the religion of everyday life' (Marx 1961, p. 384), in its exclusive attention to the level of 'appearances', and consequent neglect of their determining social relations. While the immediate appearances and 'forms of appearance' of capitalist society 'contain some part of the essential content of the relations which they mediate' (Hall 1973, p. 9) they represent this content in a distorted form. The distortion consists principally in taking (i.e., mistaking, mis-recognising) the part or the surface forms (appearances) for the whole (the 'real relations' which produce and structure the level of appearances). This is not to suggest that these levels do not have their own materiality, practices and relative autonomy (cf., Althusser 1977). We would argue with Geras (1972, p. 301) that capitalist society is necessarily characterised by a quality of opacity, and that ideology arises from the opacity of this reality, where the forms in which reality 'presents itself', or the forms of its appearance, conceal those real relations which themselves produce the appearances.

> The origin of ideological illusions is in the phenomenal forms of reality itself ... the invisibility of real relations derives from the visibility of outward appearances or forms ... this is the mechanism by which capitalist society necessarily appears to its agents as something other than it really is. (Mepham 1974, p. 103.)

The strength of ideology at a common-sense level, then, lies in its apparent justification by the perceived forms and practices of empirical social reality: Williams' 'reciprocal confirmation'. It is surely in this 'closed circle' of 'instant recognition' that *Nationwide*'s discourse moves. Its very project is 'presenting a nightly mirror to the face of Britain'. This discourse

> does not just distract attention away from real social relations, nor does it explain them away, nor does it even directly deny them; it structurally excludes them from thought – because of the very immediacy and 'visibility' of the 'natural, self-understood meanings' encountered in social life, the 'spontaneous' modes of speech and thought under capitalism . . . (Mepham 1974, p. 107.)

This network of 'given' meanings, embedded in the structure of language and common sense, is the field of discourse in and on which *Nationwide* operates – constituting and constituted by the contours of this map of dominant or preferred meanings.

Ideology then is to be understood here

> not as what is hidden and concealed but precisely as what is most open, apparent, manifest; what 'takes place in the surface and in view of all men' . . . the most obvious and 'transparent' forms of consciousness which operate in our everyday experience and ordinary language: common sense. (Hall 1977, p. 325.)

Thus the most immediately 'appearance-like' level of all – the form of spontaneous appropriation of lived relations in immediate consciousness – is itself the product of specific ideological 'work': the labour of the production of common sense.

Nationwide produces a discourse based on and in these 'spontaneous' forms of experience and it is a discourse in which the structures of class, gender and race are absent. What we see is a cast of individual characters through whose activities *Nationwide* constructs a picture of 'the British people', in their diversity. We are constituted together as members of the regional communities which make up the nation and as members of families, and in our shared concern with this domestic life is grounded *Nationwide*'s common-sense discourse. The domestic sphere, presented as a realm of leisure, is both the explicit focus of *Nationwide* discourse and the perspective from which *Nationwide* will approach other areas of concern. Given the taken-for-granted separation of the domestic from the economic/political spheres, *Nationwide* is thus able to present its own particular 'domestic' perspective as both a-political and natural: 'it's only common sense.'

Bibliography

Althusser, L. (1971), *Lenin and Philosophy*, New Left Books, London.
Althusser, L. (1977), *Essays in self-criticism*, New Left Books, London.
Alexander, S. (1976), 'Women's work in 19th Century London', in Mitchell and Oakley 1976.
Barratt, M. (1973), *Michael Barratt*, Wolfe Publishing, London.
Barthes, R. (1967), *Elements of Semiology*, Jonathan Cape, London.
Barthes, R. (1972), *Mythologies*, Paladin, London.
Beynon, H. (1976), *Working For Ford*, EP Publishing, London.
Beynon, H. and Nicholls, T. (1977), *Living with Capitalism*, Routledge and Kegan Paul, London.
Brody, R. (1976), '*Nationwide*'s contribution to the construction of the reality of everyday life', M.A. Thesis, Centre for Contemporary Cultural Studies.
Buscombe, E. (1976), '*The Sweeney*', Screen Education n.20, SEFT, London.
Cardiff, D. (1974), 'The Broadcast Interview', Polytechnic of Central London mimeo.
Conference of Socialist Economists (1976), *The Political Economy of Women*, Stage 1, London.
Coulson, Magas, Wainwright (1975), 'Women and the Class Struggle', *New Left Review*, n.89.
Connell, I. (1975), 'London Town: A kind of Television Down Your Way', CCCS mimeo.
Connell, Clarke, McDonough (1977), 'Ideology in Political Power and Social Classes', *Working Papers in Cultural Studies*, n.10.
Connell, Hall, Curti (1976), 'The Unity of Current Affairs TV', *Working Papers in Cultural Studies*, n.9.
Davidoff, L'Esperance, Newby (1976), 'Landscape with figures', in Mitchell and Oakley 1976.
Dorfman, A. and Mattelart, A. (1975), *How to Read Donald Duck*, International General, New York.
Downing, J. (1976), 'Gravediggers' Difficulties . . .', in Scase (ed.), *Industrial Society: Class, Cleavage, Control*, Arnold, London, 1976.
Engels, F. (1975), *Origin of the Family*, Pathfinder, London.
Gerbner, G. (1964), 'Ideological Tendencies in Political Reporting', in *Journalism Quarterly*, Vol. 41, n.4.
Geras, N. (1972), 'Marx and the Critique of Political Economy', in Blackburn (ed.), *Ideology in Social Science*, Fontana, London, 1972.
Gillman, P. (1975), 'Nation at Large', *Sunday Times*, 2/3/75.
Gramsci, A. (1971), *Prison Notebooks*, Lawrence and Wishart, London.
Hall, C. (1974), 'The History of the Housewife', *Spare Rib* n.26.
Hall, S. (1972), 'The Determinations of News Photographs', *Working Papers in Cultural Studies*, n.3.
Hall, S. (1973), 'Signification and Ideologies', CCCS mimeo.
Hall, S. (1977), 'Culture and the Ideological Effect', in Curran et al. (eds.), *Mass Communications and Society*, Arnold, 1977.
Hall, Lumley, McLellan (1977), 'Politics & Ideology: Gramsci', *Working Papers in Cultural Studies*, n.10.
Halliday, M. (1973), *Explorations in the Function of Language*, Arnold, London.
Harris, N. (1971), *Beliefs in Society*, Penguin, Harmondsworth.
Hoggart, R. (1957), *The Uses of Literacy*, Penguin, Harmondsworth.
Heath, S. and Skirrow, G. (1977), 'Television: a world in action', *Screen* Vol. 18, n.2.
Kracauer, S. (1952), 'The Challenge of Qualitative Analysis', *Public Opinion Quarterly*, Winter 1952.
Lane, T. (1974), *The Union Makes us Strong*, Arrow, London.
Lloyd, A. L. (1969), *Folk Song in England*, Panther, London.
Marx, K. (1976), *Capital* Vol. 1, Penguin, Harmondsworth.
Marx, K. (1961), *Capital* Vol. 3, Lawrence and Wishart, London.
Marx, K. (1973), *Grundrisse*, Penguin, Harmondsworth.
Mattelart, M. (1975), 'Chile: the feminist side of the coup – when bourgeois women take to the streets', *Casa de las Americas*, Jan. 1975.

Mepham, J. (1974), 'The Theory of Ideology in *Capital*', *Working Papers in Cultural Studies*, n.6.

Millett, K. (1971), *Sexual Politics*, Hart Davis, London.

Mitchell, J. and Oakley, A. (1976), *The Rights and Wrongs of Women*, Penguin, Harmondsworth.

Morley, D. (1976), 'Industrial Conflict and the Mass Media', *Sociological Review*, May 1976.

Nicholls, T. and Armstrong, P. (1976), *Workers Divided*, Fontana, London.

Nowell-Smith, G. (1974), 'Common Sense', *Radical Philosophy*, Spring 1974.

Parkin, F. (1972), *Class Inequality and Political Order*, Paladin, London.

Poulantzas, N. (1975), *Political Power and Social Classes*, New Left Books, London.

Robey, D. (ed.) (1973), *Structuralism*, Oxford University Press, London.

Rowbottham, S. (1973), *Woman's Consciousness, Man's World*, Penguin, Harmondsworth.

Smith, A. (1975), *Paper Voices*, Chatto and Windus, London.

Thompson, E. (1977), 'Happy Families', *New Society*, 8/9/77.

Williams, R. (1973), 'Base and Superstructure', *New Left Review*, n.82.

Williams, R. (1975), *Keywords*, Fontana, London.

Williams, R. (1976), *The Country and the City*, Fontana, London.

Williamson, J. (1978), *Decoding Advertisements*, Boyars, London.

Wilson, E. (1977), *Women and the Welfare State*, Tavistock, London.

Winship, J. (1978), 'Woman', in *Women Take Issue*, CCCS/Hutchinson, London, 1978.

Zaretsky, E. (1976), *Capitalism, the Family and Personal Life*, Pluto Press, London.